## Checking the key features of a moss

### Capillary Thread-moss
*Bryum capillare*

**HABITAT** Be aware of your surroundings a
be found in certain types of habitat.
**WHERE TO LOOK** Mosses and liverworts a
such as steep-sided slopes, shaded rock:
Some mosses and liverworts are also ea
**DESCRIPTION** Look at the colour, size and :
they grow in cushions or individual plants or a mat of
creeping tendrils? Separate out individual shoots and
branches. Investigate individual leaves. Check to see
if capsules are present and what shape they are.
Do capsules have a calyptra (see below)?
**SIMILAR SPECIES** Here you will find information
about similar species.

**Liverworts** – Often found in dark and damp areas they look more primitive than mosses and lack a leaf nerve.
The two main forms are: leafy liverworts which are often very flat with leaves organised in parallel rows along
the shoot; and thallose liverworts which have a thick, flat, slimy, green thallus which grows outward from a
central point. A thallus can often have forked or cut edges which are important for identification. Fruiting
liverworts have round capsules held on a stalk (seta).

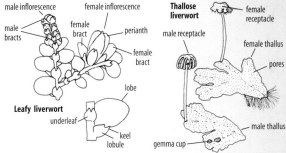

**Mosses** – Look like miniature green leafy plants and have two main types: acrocarps, which are tufted mosses
which grow from a central point often forming circular cushions; and pleurocarps, which have longer shoots and are
more tendril-like, often with branches. Fruiting mosses have a capsule usually held on a seta. The tip of a capsule is
covered by a calyptra (see below) which drops off as the capsule matures.

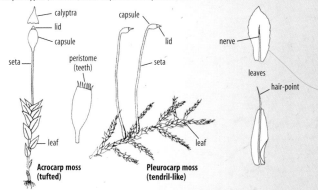

### What you need
To identify mosses it is important to have a small field magnifying glass (called a hand lens). For mosses in this book a
hand lens with ×10 magnification is suitable. A pen and paper are also useful to note down any habitat information
and key features. A little spray bottle full of water is useful for spraying on dry mosses to help them open up.

Mosses and liverworts can be found in a wide variety of habitats, growing on the ground in woodland and grassland, on rocks and walls, or on living and dead wood. Some may favour a particular habitat or type of tree. The main habitats, and some of the best places to look locally, are mentioned here.

# Grassland and heathland

The chalk and limestone grassland of the Chilterns, Cotswolds and the Downs, and the acid grassland and heathlands of Berkshire hold a good number of both common and rare mosses and liverworts. Some of the best sites to visit are – **Berks:** Greenham Common, Snelsmore Common, and Decoy Heath, Inkpen Common and Wildmoor Heath nature reserves; **Bucks:** Dancersend nature reserve and Grangelands; **Oxon:** Aston Rowant National Nature Reserve, Watlington Hill, and Hartslock and Warburg nature reserves. LOOK FOR Common Threadwort, Tumid Notchwort, Inflated Notchwort, Crenulated Flapwort, Bristly Haircap, Juniper Haircap, Clay Earth-moss, Taper-leaved Earth-moss, Redshank, Dwarf Swan-neck Moss, Heath Star-moss, Rock Pocket-moss, Crisp Beardless-moss, Curly Crisp-moss, Bonfire-moss, Rose-moss, Nodding Thread-moss, Comb-moss, Red-stemmed Feather-moss, Springy Turf-moss

# Arable land

Arable land seems an unlikely habitat to look for mosses, but it is always worth checking for the many small mosses that are found on this unpromising-looking habitat, particularly around field edges and in stubble fields.
LOOK FOR Common Crystalwort, Field Forklet-moss, Common Pottia, Cuspidate Earth-moss, Upright Pottia, Common Bladder-moss, Bicoloured Bryum, Silver-moss

# Quarries, bare chalk, rocks and walls

Quarries, rocks and walls, particularly in chalk and limestone areas, are rich in mosses that can survive these often dry habitats. Gravestones in churchyards are also worth looking at. Some of the best sites to visit are – **Berks**: Hurley Chalk Pit nature reserve; **Bucks:** Pulpit Hill; **Oxon:** Ardley Quarry, Chinnor Hill, Dry Sandford Pit, Hitchcopse Pit and Hook Norton Cutting nature reserves and Kirtlington Quarry. LOOK FOR Top Notchwort, Wall Scalewort, Common Pincushion, Variable Forklet-moss, Beard-mosses, Aloe-mosses, Wall Screw-moss, Sand-hill Screw-moss, Intermediate Screw-moss, Thickpoint Grimmia, Grey-cushioned Grimmia, Extinguisher-mosses, Capillary Thread-moss, Silver-moss, Anomalous Bristle-moss, Rambling Tail-moss, Silky Wall Feather-moss, Whitish Feather-moss

# Marshes, fens and bogs

These wetland habitats hold some of the more uncommon mosses and liverworts found in our region. Fens are a rare habitat, found mainly in the Cothill area of Oxfordshire, whereas bogs are mainly restricted to Berkshire. Some of the best sites to visit are – **Berks:** Snelsmore Common, and Sole Common Pond and Wildmoor Heath nature reserves; **Oxon:** Dry Sandford Pit and Parsonage Moor nature reserves. LOOK FOR Inflated Notchwort, Overleaf Pellia, Endive Pellia, Greasewort, Bog-mosses, Common Haircap, Maidenhair Pocket-moss, Marsh Bryum, Bog Bead-moss, Tree-moss, Curled Hook-moss, Yellow Starry Feather-moss, Intermediate Hook-moss, Pointed Spear-moss

# Rivers and streams

Riverbanks and stream sides, particularly in the flood zones, locks and weirs, have their special mosses, some often submerged. Most riversides are worth a look at in our area. LOOK FOR Overleaf Pellia, Endive Pellia, Great Scented Liverwort, Pointed Lattice-moss, Water Screw-moss, Hooded Bristle-moss, Many-fruited Leskea

# Woodland

Woodland is by far the richest habitat for mosses and liverworts. From the woodland floor to the trees themselves, mosses find a niche somewhere here. Woodlands found in the chalk and limestone districts can have a different range of species from those on the more acidic soils of Berkshire. Some species of tree are worth a closer look at, especially ash, elder, field maple and willow, as they are particularly rich is mosses. Some of the best sites to visit are – **Berks:** Bowdown Woods and Moor Copse nature reserves, Windsor Great Park; **Bucks:** Bernwood Forest, Burnham Beeches, Chiltern beechwoods, and Finemere Wood, Millfield Wood and Rushbeds Wood nature reserves; **Oxon:** Chiltern beechwoods, Shotover Country Park, Whitehill Wood, Wychwood, and Sydlings Copse and Warburg nature reserves. LOOK FOR Creeping Fingerwort, Two-horned Pincerwort, White Earwort, Bifid Crestwort, Variable-leaved Crestwort, Greater Featherwort, Even Scalewort, Wall Scalewort, Dilated Scalewort, Fairy Beads, Veilworts, Bank Haircap, Common Smoothcap, Pellucid Four-tooth Moss, Common Pincushion, Silky Forklet-moss, Broom Fork-moss, Greater Fork-moss, Large White-moss, Pocket-mosses, Small Hairy Screw-moss, Marble Screw-moss, Rock-bristles, Cape Thread-moss, Thyme-mosses, Drumsticks, Yoke-mosses, Bristle-mosses, Pincushions, Lateral Cryphaea, Flat Neckera, Feather-mosses, Rambling Tail-moss, Common Tamarisk-moss, Mouse-tail Moss, Silk-mosses, Flat-brocade Moss, Plait-mosses, Big Shaggy-moss

## Knothole Yoke-moss
*Zygodon forsteri*

One of our rarest mosses, the Knothole Yoke-moss, is protected by law and is found at just three sites in Britain – Epping Forest, the New Forest and, in our area, at Burnham Beeches in Bucks. It grows in knotholes in the trunks and gnarled roots of ancient beech trees.

5mm

## What to look for

The liverworts (pp.5–19) and mosses (pp.20–71) described in this section can all be found locally and have been chosen because of their distinctive features. Many are common, some less often seen. Some are restricted to a particular habitat or associated with a type of tree. Similar species are also mentioned.

# Creeping Fingerwort
*Lepidozia reptans*

**HABITAT** Woodland
**WHERE TO LOOK** Low to the ground in woodlands on damp acid soils, often on tree trunks and rotting stumps
**DESCRIPTION** A small yellowish-green to dark green, branched, creeping liverwort, with shoots 1–2cm long; leaves about 0.5mm long, hand shaped with 4 finger-like projections
**SIMILAR SPECIES** **Bristly Fingerwort** *Kurzia pauciflora* is a much smaller liverwort whose leaves are divided to the base into 3 or 4 lobes; usually intermixed with *Sphagnum* mosses in valley bogs

Detail of leaves

1mm

5mm

5

# Common Pouchwort
*Calypogeia fissa*

**HABITAT** Woodland and valley bogs
**WHERE TO LOOK** On acid banks in woodland and on peat and *Sphagnum* mosses in valley bogs
**DESCRIPTION** The commonest *Calypogeia* liverwort, often growing very flat to the ground; leaves in 2 rows, slightly overlapping; leaf shape is rounded/pointed, some with shallow notches that do not diverge; pale green gemmae usually occur at shoot tips
**SIMILAR SPECIES** **Mueller's Pouchwort** *Calypogeia muelleriana* has all leaves rounded, underleaves with shallow notches; **Notched Pouchwort** *Calypogeia arguta* has all leaves tipped with divergent teeth

Detail of leaves with shallow notches

2mm

3mm

# Two-horned Pincerwort
*Cephalozia bicuspidata*

**HABITAT** Damp acid woodland, peat and rotting wood
**WHERE TO LOOK** Found on banks, earth and sides of ditches as
   pure patches or growing amongst other liverworts and mosses
**DESCRIPTION** A tiny green liverwort with translucent, pointed
   bilobed leaves less than 1mm wide; leaves are joined diagonally
   to the stem; no underleaves; female shoots are prominent with
   perianths up to 3mm long
**SIMILAR SPECIES** **Forcipated Pincerwort** *Cephalozia connivens*
   grows in *Sphagnum* bogs

Detail of dry leaves

5mm

6

# Rustwort
*Nowellia curvifolia*

**HABITAT** Woodland
**WHERE TO LOOK** Rare, on rotting wood and logs; found in the
   north and west of Britain, this liverwort is spreading slowly into
   our area
**DESCRIPTION** Unmistakeable liverwort with its rusty-crimson
   shoots (0.5–1mm wide) and green shoot tips; leaves (up to
   1mm wide) concave with two long curved teeth
**SIMILAR SPECIES** Unlikely to be confused with other species

Detail of leaves

4mm

# Common Threadwort
*Cephaloziella divaricata*

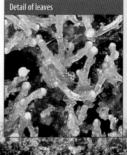

Detail of leaves

1mm

**HABITAT** Damp heathy habitats that can periodically dry out
**WHERE TO LOOK** Berkshire heathlands, Decoy Heath, near
  Aldermaston is especially good
**DESCRIPTION** A tiny, patch-forming, slender green or brownish
  liverwort; separate male and female plants often grow
  intermixed; shoots up to 0.5mm wide with bilobed leaves only
  0.2mm long; leaf tips pinched together
**SIMILAR SPECIES** **Hampe's Threadwort** *Cephaloziella hampeana*
  and **Red Threadwort** *Cephaloziella rubella* are
  both similar but tend to grow in damper
  areas or on rotting logs

5mm

# Tumid Notchwort
*Lophozia ventricosa*

Detail of leaves with gemmae

2mm

**HABITAT** Heathland and pine plantations
**WHERE TO LOOK** Found in Berks on damp heathy ground, acid
  banks and occasionally in bogs
**DESCRIPTION** A small, opaque, green liverwort with shoots 1–
  2mm wide; leaves bilobed (1–1.5mm long) with clusters of
  green gemmae at tips; no underleaves
**SIMILAR SPECIES** **Lesser Notchwort** *Lophozia bicrenata*, a rare
  plant of heathland in Berks and acid soil in the Chilterns,
  has orange-brown gemmae on leaves

4mm

# Top Notchwort
*Leiocolea turbinata*

Detail of leaves

**HABITAT** Chalk pits and bare chalk in woodland and grassland
**WHERE TO LOOK** Steep, bare slopes on chalk, mainly in the Chilterns
**DESCRIPTION** Although tiny, this pale green liverwort can form mats covering large areas of bare chalk; shoots slender (0.5–1.5mm wide) with widely spaced, rounded bilobed leaves (1mm long), narrowed at leaf base; no underleaves; female plants with tubular perianths (see picture below)
**SIMILAR SPECIES Scarce Notchwort** *Leiocolea badensis*, also found on chalk, is much rarer and has a wider leaf base

5mm

# Inflated Notchwort
*Gymnocolea inflata*

Detail of leaves

**HABITAT** Acid habitats including heathland, bogs and peaty soil in conifer plantations
**WHERE TO LOOK** Bare soil on wet heathland and around edges of peaty pools, particular abundant under heather at Decoy Heath
**DESCRIPTION** A small green to dark green (sometimes almost blackish) liverwort with narrow shoots (to 2mm wide); rounded bilobed leaves (1mm long) with V-shaped notch; female plants have conspicuous, inflated perianths, like small, elongated balloons (see picture below)
**SIMILAR SPECIES** Unlikely to be confused with other species

4mm

# Crenulated Flapwort
*Solenostoma gracillimum*

Detail of perianths

3mm

**HABITAT** Acid woodland rides, clay and sandy areas and heathland
**WHERE TO LOOK** Open, bare areas on clay or acid soils, ditch sides and woodland rides
**DESCRIPTION** Green to rusty liverwort, forming colonies of male and female plants; leaves round (1mm wide) with a thickened border (best seen with hand lens); no underleaves; male plants with slender shoots, female plants with shoots to 2mm wide
**SIMILAR SPECIES** **Ladder Flapwort** *Nardia scalaris*, found in the same habitats, is similar in shape but has peg-like underleaves (seen with a hand lens) and is much rarer

3mm

# White Earwort
*Diplophyllum albicans*

Underside of leaves

5mm

**HABITAT** Acid soils in woodland and heathy areas
**WHERE TO LOOK** Acid woodland banks in Berks and the Chilterns
**DESCRIPTION** Often forming large patches of male and female plants, green to brownish when wet, whitish-green when dry, with shoots up to 3.5mm wide and often several cm long; leaves (0.8mm wide × 1.8mm long) with long, rounded lobes, colourless cells in middle of leaf (seen with a hand lens); leaves flat when wet, curled up when dry
**SIMILAR SPECIES** Unlikely to be confused with other species

3mm

# Grove Earwort
*Scapania nemorea*

HABITAT Woodland
WHERE TO LOOK On humid banks and tree stumps along woodland
    rides, rare in Berks and the Chilterns
DESCRIPTION A large, green liverwort with dense, overlapping
    shoots (1.5–5mm wide) that can be several cm long; leaves
    lobed (to 2.5mm long), broadly rounded and bordered with
    long teeth; brown gemmae form in clusters on leaf lobes
SIMILAR SPECIES **Heath Earwort** *Scapania irrigua*, another rare
    liverwort of humid woodland lacks the brown gemmae
    and has a pointed leaf with smoother margins;
    **Rough Earwort** *Scapania aspera* is a
    rare liverwort of chalk grassland
    on the Chiltern escarpment

Detail of leaves with brown gemmae

5mm

# Bifid Crestwort
*Lophocolea bidentata*

HABITAT Woodland, grassland and heathland
WHERE TO LOOK The commonest leafy liverwort, found on the
    ground, tree bases and rotting wood
DESCRIPTION An aromatic, translucent, pale green liverwort with
    shoots (2–4mm wide) to several cm long; leaves (2mm long)
    bilobed, with lobes long and narrowly pointed
SIMILAR SPECIES **Variable-leaved Crestwort** *Lophocolea
heterophylla*, equally common, has a mixture of unlobed and
    lobed leaves; **Southern Crestwort** *Lophocolea
semiteres*, a pale green, invasive species
    from the southern hemisphere, is
    spreading on heathland
    at Greenham Common

Capsules

5mm

# St Winifred's Moss
## *Chiloscyphus polyanthos*

**HABITAT** Wet ground in acid woodland and alder carr
**WHERE TO LOOK** Streamsides, mud and tree roots
**DESCRIPTION** A mat-forming, green, translucent liverwort with
  shoots 1.5–4.5mm wide; leaves (2mm long) slightly alternate,
  rounded, with the leaf base running onto the stem; underleaves
  small, narrow and bilobed; female plant perianth lobes
  undivided and hardly toothed (seen with a hand lens)
**SIMILAR SPECIES Pale Liverwort** *Chiloscyphus pallescens*, very
  similar but paler, with female perianth lobes toothed,
  is found on wet clay banks, damp
  woodland tracks and fen

Detail of leaves

2mm

5mm

11

# Greater Featherwort
## *Plagiochila asplenioides*

**HABITAT** Woodland
**WHERE TO LOOK** Woodland banks and streamsides
**DESCRIPTION** A large leafy liverwort with stems to 12cm long and
  5–9mm wide; leaves (2.5–4.5mm wide and long) rounded
  with small teeth, are closely spaced and overlap in neat rows up
  the stem; underleaves are minute and barely visible
**SIMILAR SPECIES Lesser Featherwort** *Plagiochila porelloides*,
  found on woodland banks on chalk and limestone, is similar in
  shape but is smaller, with leaves to 3mm long

Detail of leaves

5mm

8mm

# Even Scalewort
*Radula complanata*

**HABITAT** Sheltered woodland, scrub and hedgerows
**WHERE TO LOOK** Found on trees and shrubs, especially on ash,
elder, willow and field maple
**DESCRIPTION** An epiphytic, yellowish-green liverwort (to 3cm
long), growing in flat patches; bilobed leaves (1.5mm wide),
rounded and overlapping (smaller lobule folded underneath),
frequently with gemmae along the leaf margin; perianths long
and flat
**SIMILAR SPECIES** Unlikely to be confused with other species

Perianths with capsules

2mm

12

# Wall Scalewort
*Porella platyphylla*

**HABITAT** Woodland and limestone walls
**WHERE TO LOOK** Bases of trees, particularly ash and field maple in
ancient woodland, and in the Chilterns on beech; also found on
tops of limestone walls
**DESCRIPTION** A large, mid- to dark green, leafy liverwort, growing
in large patches or wefts of pinnate shoots up to 3cm across
and several cm long; leaves to 2mm wide; blunt lobules with
upturned edges at the base of leaf and a row of underleaves
can be seen on underside of shoots
**SIMILAR SPECIES** Unlikely to be confused with
other species

Detail of leaves

20mm

# Dilated Scalewort
*Frullania dilitata*

**HABITAT** Woodland and scrub
**WHERE TO LOOK** A very common liverwort found on trunks and branches of a variety of trees, especially ash and willow
**DESCRIPTION** A greenish to reddish-brown, leafy liverwort with shoots to 1.5mm wide, growing in flat (often extensive) patches; leaves with rounded lobes (1mm wide), and smaller lobules and underleaves (seen on the underside); male shoots narrow, female shoots with warty perianths
**SIMILAR SPECIES** Unlikely to be confused with other species

Perianths and dehesced capsule

3mm

8mm

# Fairy Beads
*Microlejeunea ulicina*

**HABITAT** Woodland
**WHERE TO LOOK** Found on tree trunks in humid, sheltered woodland
**DESCRIPTION** A tiny, pale green, leafy liverwort growing in patches of string-like shoots, hard to spot on tree trunks as it is so small (shoots to 6mm long and 0.3mm wide); leaves minute (0.15–0.25mm wide), oval with a bluntly pointed tip and bilobed underleaves (difficult to see, even with a hand lens)
**SIMILAR SPECIES** The rare **Minute Pouncewort** *Cololejeunea minutissima* (see p.14) looks similar, but is slightly smaller and has no underleaves

Detail of leaves

2mm

5mm

# Minute Pouncewort
*Cololejeunea minutissima*

**HABITAT** Woodland
**WHERE TO LOOK** A rare liverwort found on tree trunks (often at the base) in humid places; seems to be spreading
**DESCRIPTION** A tiny, pale green, leafy liverwort, forming dense patches of slender shoots (to 4mm long and 0.5mm wide); leaves minute (up to 0.2mm long), round, without underleaves; perianths 5-keeled (looking like 5-pointed stars)
**SIMILAR SPECIES** **Fairy Beads** *Microlejeunea ulicina* (see p.13) is similar in size and has underleaves

Detail of leaves and perianths

3mm

# Overleaf Pellia
*Pellia epiphylla*

**HABITAT** Wet woodland, marshes, stream and riverbanks
**WHERE TO LOOK** On the ground (preferring neutral to acid soils) in wet woodland and marshes, sides of ditches, stream and riverbanks
**DESCRIPTION** Medium-sized, dark green (sometimes purplish tinged), thallose liverwort; thallus (to 1cm wide) sparingly branched; capsules (emerging from a vertical flap) common, on long seta
**SIMILAR SPECIES** **Endive Pellia** *Pellia endiviifolia* (see p.15) has separate male and female plants and grows in more calcareous sites

Detail of thallus and capsules

20mm

# Endive Pellia
*Pellia endiviifolia*

**HABITAT** Wet woodland, flushes, fens, springs, quarry floors, stream and riverbanks
**WHERE TO LOOK** Found on the ground in damp or wet situations in calcareous areas
**DESCRIPTION** Medium-sized, green to blackish-green, thallose liverwort (to 1cm wide) with separate male and female plants; thallus develops many narrow branches (like miniature endive leaves) at the tip (see detail picture) in autumn and early winter; vertical tube, with toothed mouth, surrounds female organ
**SIMILAR SPECIES** Overleaf Pellia
*Pellia epiphylla* (see p.14)

Detail of male thallus

7.5mm

15mm

# Greasewort
*Aneura pinguis*

**HABITAT** Calcareous flushes, springs and fens
**WHERE TO LOOK** An uncommon liverwort found on the ground in wet, calcareous habitats, especially in the springs and fens near Abingdon in Oxfordshire
**DESCRIPTION** A greasy looking, mid-green thallose liverwort, very variable in size (from 1–8cm long); in highly calcareous sites the liverwort can be hardened with calcium; thallus thick with wavy margin, capsules emerge from sides of thallus
**SIMILAR SPECIES** Endive Pellia (see above); Overleaf Pellia
*Pellia epiphylla* (see p.14)

Developing capsules

10mm

8mm

# Blueish Veilwort
*Metzgeria violacea*

Detail of dry thallus with gemmae

**HABITAT** Woodland and scrub
**WHERE TO LOOK** Found on branches and twigs of trees, especially willow, elder, ash and hazel
**DESCRIPTION** A small, yellowish-green (turning blueish in old plants), thallose liverwort, forming patches on bark; thallus (1mm wide) with prominent midrib and conspicuous, gemmae-bearing branches (gemmae clustered at branch tips) sticking out from the patch; gemmae can wash off after heavy rain
**SIMILAR SPECIES** **Whiskered Veilwort** (see below) is similar but has gemmae along the margins of the thallus branch; **Forked Veilwort** *Metzgeria furcata* (see p.17) is larger and does not have gemmae

8mm

# Whiskered Veilwort
*Metzgeria consanguinea*

Detail of thallus with gemmae

**HABITAT** Humid woodland and scrub
**WHERE TO LOOK** Found on branches and twigs of trees, especially willow, elder, ash and field maple and on alder trunks
**DESCRIPTION** A small, yellowish-green, thallose liverwort, forming patches on bark; thallus (1mm wide) with prominent midrib and conspicuous, gemmae-bearing branches (gemmae along margins of branch) sticking out from the patch; gemmae can wash off after heavy rain
**SIMILAR SPECIES** **Blueish Veilwort** (see above) has gemmae at the branch tips; **Forked Veilwort** *Metzgeria furcata* (see p.17) does not have gemmae

5mm

# Forked Veilwort
*Metzgeria furcata*

**HABITAT** Woodland, scrub, hedgerows and limestone walls
**WHERE TO LOOK** A common thallose liverwort, found on trunks
and branches of a wide variety of trees, especially ash, willow,
elder and field maple; also rarely on limestone walls
**DESCRIPTION** A small, yellowish-green, thallose liverwort,
forming patches on bark; thallus (1–1.5mm wide) forked at
tip, with prominent, thick midrib
**SIMILAR SPECIES Blueish Veilwort** *Metzgeria violacea* (see p.16)
and **Whiskered Veilwort** *Metzgeria consanguinea*
(see p.16) both have gemmae-bearing
thallus branches

Wet thallus showing thick midrib

4mm

8mm

17

# Micheli's Balloonwort
*Sphaerocarpos michelii*

**HABITAT** Neglected gardens, plant nurseries and arable fields
**WHERE TO LOOK** A rare liverwort, found on neutral or sandy soils
**DESCRIPTION** An odd-looking, thallose liverwort with densely
packed, balloon-like structures surrounding sex organs; female
plants (up to 2cm across) with inflated, balloon-like structure
1–1.75mm in diameter; male plants inconspicuous (5mm
across), often hidden by female plants growing over them
**SIMILAR SPECIES** Unlikely to be confused with other species

Detail of balloon-like structures

1.5mm

3mm

# Crescent-cup Liverwort
*Lunularia cruciata*

**HABITAT** Gardens, man-made habitats, stream and riverbanks
**WHERE TO LOOK** Found on garden paths, bases of walls, in flower
   pots and greenhouses, shady lanes, steambanks and riverbanks
**DESCRIPTION** A large, shiny green, branching, thallose liverwort;
   thallus (12mm wide) covered in tiny, conspicuous air pores;
   crescent-shaped cups with green gemmae form on the thallus
**SIMILAR SPECIES** **Common Liverwort** *Marchantia polymorpha*
   subsp. *ruderalis* (see p.19

Crescent-shaped gemmae cups

8mm

# Great Scented Liverwort
*Conocephalum conicum*

**HABITAT** Steambanks and riverbanks, locks and weirs, fens and
   woodland springs
**WHERE TO LOOK** A common thallose liverwort found on the shady
   banks of streams and rivers, ditchsides and on the sides of locks
   and weirs, and in fens and woodland springs
**DESCRIPTION** A very large, aromatic, green to dark green, thallose
   liverwort, forming extensive patches; thallus large (to 17mm
   wide), flat and leathery, shiny, covered in tiny, conspicuous,
   air pores
**SIMILAR SPECIES** Unlikely to be confused
   with other species

Detail of thallus

15mm

# Common Liverwort
*Marchantia polymorpha* subsp. *ruderalis*

Detail of female receptacle

5mm

**HABITAT** Gardens, man-made habitats, stream and riverbanks
**WHERE TO LOOK** Found on garden paths, bases of walls, in flower pots and greenhouses, shady lanes, and occasionally on steambanks and riverbanks
**DESCRIPTION** A large, green, branching, thallose liverwort; thallus (15mm wide) with blackish line running down centre and covered in tiny air pores; circular cups with green gemmae form on the thallus; male plants have stalked, flat-topped, disc-like receptacle, female plants have receptacles with finger-like lobes
**SIMILAR SPECIES Crescent-cup Liverwort**
*Lunularia cruciata* (see p.18)) grows
in the same habitats, but
has crescent-shaped
gemmae cups

8mm

19

# Common Crystalwort
*Riccia sorocarpa*

Detail of thallus with capsule

2.5mm

**HABITAT** Arable fields, bare soils and woodland rides
**WHERE TO LOOK** A decreasing liverwort found on the ground in arable fields, bare muddy soil and damp woodland rides
**DESCRIPTION** A grey-green, thallose liverwort, forming irregular rosettes (to 2cm in diameter); thallus branches (2–2.5mm wide) with conspicuous V-shaped groove and colourless margin; capsules are seen on decaying parts of thallus
**SIMILAR SPECIES Glaucous Crystalwort** *Riccia glauca* has thallus branches with shallow, flat groove; **Least Crystalwort** *Riccia subbifurca*, much smaller, is found on bare soil in wet heath on Greenham Common in Berks

5mm

# Papillose Bog-moss
*Sphagnum papillosum*

Capitulum

**HABITAT** Peat bogs
**WHERE TO LOOK** Valley bogs and inundated areas – sites include Snelsmore Common and Wildmoor Heath in Berks
**DESCRIPTION** A hummock-forming robust species with short, chunky tendrils, and equally short and chunky vegetative branches at the head of the plant (capitulum); whole plant often brown to ochre in colour; blunt-tipped leaf shoots with a small leafy hood
**SIMILAR SPECIES** **Blunt-leaved Bog-moss** (see below) is not as uniform in colour, whilst **Magellanic Bog-moss** *Sphagnum magellanicum* (also found in valley bogs in Berks) is often red to green in colour

5mm

# Blunt-leaved Bog-moss
*Sphagnum palustre*

Capitulum

**HABITAT** Inundated areas, wet woodlands, slow-running streams and ditches
**WHERE TO LOOK** Found on many damp and slightly enriched sites, among inundated vegetation
**DESCRIPTION** Robust bog-moss that does not float like some other *Sphagnum* species; variable in colour, often with a distinctly brown or ochre capitulum and much paler tendrils, it can also be green or tinted pink (never red); often with 2–3 spreading and up to 4 drooping branches; leaves are large, narrow and blunt
**SIMILAR SPECIES** **Papillose Bog-moss** (see above)

8mm

# Red Bog-moss
*Sphagnum capillifolium* subsp. *rubellum*

Capitulum

3mm

**HABITAT** Valley bogs and wet heathland
**WHERE TO LOOK** Regularly inundated areas in wet heathland and
valley bogs in Berks, often among other *Sphagnum* species.
**DESCRIPTION** A red bog-moss forming soft hummocks and
blankets; capitulum is quite flat topped, branching tendrils are
fine-leaved and overlapping; stem leaves slightly rounded at
tip and less than 1.2mm long.
**SIMILAR SPECIES Magellanic Bog-moss** *Sphagnum magellanicum*
is wine red to red-green in colour and has shorter branches and
fatter leaves; **Lustrous Bog-moss** *Sphagnum
subnitens* is a pinkish-green and
often has a green capitulum

6mm

# Compact Bog-moss
*Sphagnum compactum*

Detail of capitulum

1.5mm

**HABITAT** Wet heathland and conifer plantations
**WHERE TO LOOK** Uncommon bog-moss found in open areas and
disturbed wet ground at a few sites in Berks
**DESCRIPTION** A compact moss, forming dense mats of pale
yellow, gold and brown colours, sometimes looser, spreading
plants are visible, with large inflated leaves; capitulum difficult
to distinguish through compact branches; leaves large and
folded inwards at the edges with a blunt leaf tip; stem leaves
minute on a blackish stem
**SIMILAR SPECIES** Unlikely to be confused with
other species

3mm

# Bank Haircap
*Polytrichastrum formosum*

**HABITAT** Broadleaved woodlands, hedge banks and heathland
**WHERE TO LOOK** A common moss of oak and beech woodlands on acid soils in shady, sheltered areas
**DESCRIPTION** Large plants growing 5–10cm tall; leaves long (1cm long), dark green, formed in a spiral along the main stem; capsules 5–6-angled on a seta up to 7–8cm long
**SIMILAR SPECIES** **Common Haircap** (see below) is a larger plant found in damper habitats

Detail of leaves and capsule

15mm

# Common Haircap
*Polytrichum commune*

**HABITAT** Heathland, wet acid woodland and bogs
**WHERE TO LOOK** Abundant in damp, acidic areas such as ditches, pond margins, wet heath and bogs
**DESCRIPTION** Large plants forming hummocks or turfs, with shoots usually 20cm tall; leaves triangular (8–12mm), dark to light green, formed in a spiral along the main stem, appearing star-like from above; leaves spread out along the stem when wet and roll up when dry; young capsules covered in hairy, golden calyptra, distinctive mature capsules box-shaped, 4-angled, on a long (up to 12cm) seta
**SIMILAR SPECIES** **Bank Haircap** (see above)

Detail of leaves

30mm

# Bristly Haircap
*Polytrichum piliferum*

**HABITAT** Heathland and acid woodland
**WHERE TO LOOK** Sandy/gravelly areas on dry, acidic soils, often
found in open patches of heath (e.g. burnt areas)
**DESCRIPTION** Short, yellow-green to greyish-green moss (2–4cm),
male plant shoots form a distinctive red 'floret' in spring; thick
leaves (3mm long), sometimes with a yellow-red margin, end in
a distinctive, curving, translucent hair point; leaves curl upwards
when dry and spread (but still curve upwards) when wet;
capsules (4–5-angled when mature) on a 1–3cm long, red seta
**SIMILAR SPECIES Juniper Haircap** (see below),
found in similar habitats, is larger and
has sharply pointed leaves
with no hair point

Male 'florets'

5mm

15mm

# Juniper Haircap
*Polytrichum juniperinum*

Male 'florets'

8mm

**HABITAT** Heathland and acid woodland
**WHERE TO LOOK** A common moss of dry, acidic soils, often found
in open patches of heath (e.g. burnt areas) and along
pathways
**DESCRIPTION** Similar in shape to Bristly Haircap, but slightly
larger and more blue-green in colour; male plant shoots
display a distinctive orange 'floret' through spring; leaves (up
to 1cm long) straight and sharp (appearing star-like from
above) with no hair point; capsules (usually 4-angled when
mature) on a 2–5cm long, reddish seta
**SIMILAR SPECIES Bristly Haircap** (see above)

20mm

# Common Smoothcap
*Atrichum undulatum*

Detail of leaves

**HABITAT** Woodlands
**WHERE TO LOOK** A common moss of broadleaved woodlands, often in shady areas and on open soil and banks.
**DESCRIPTION** Medium to large, dark green, rosette-forming moss (to 7cm); leaves tongue-shaped (up to 1cm long), widest nearer the tip; distinctive ripples wave across the leaves (best seen through a hand lens), which are softer when wet and more rigid when dry; leaf margins are toothed with double teeth (seen through a hand lens); capsules long on a red-green seta; calyptra smooth, claw-like
**SIMILAR SPECIES** Unlikely to be confused with other species

15mm

# Pellucid Four-tooth Moss
*Tetraphis pellucida*

Non-fertile shoot tips with gemmae

**HABITAT** Woodland and acid grassland
**WHERE TO LOOK** Low to the ground in woodlands on acid soils, often on tree trunks and rotting stumps and bark
**DESCRIPTION** A small, slender plant often appearing dark green from a distance with short stems (0.5–1cm); small oval leaves on branches which are held upright; the most distinctive feature is the non-fertile shoot tip terminating in a cup, filled with small green gemmae; capsules cylindrical, with 4 triangular peristome teeth
**SIMILAR SPECIES** Unlikely to be confused with other species

8mm

# Clay Earth-moss
*Archidium alternifolium*

**HABITAT** Heathland and acid woodland rides
**WHERE TO LOOK** An uncommon moss of open and moist acidic and clayey soils and rutted woodland rides; large patches are found on Greenham Common and Decoy Heath in Berks
**DESCRIPTION** Small moss forming distinctive khaki-green, turf-like mats of shoots 2cm high, plants appear wavy (like short hair growing from the soil); leaves very small (1–2mm), triangular and short, and held at an angle away from the stem (seen through a hand lens); spherical capsules occasional, hidden at base of leaves
**SIMILAR SPECIES Taper-leaved Earth-moss** (see below), similar in size, often grows in the same places

Detail of leaves

5mm

10mm

# Taper-leaved Earth-moss
*Pleuridium acuminatum*

**HABITAT** Heathland and acid woodland rides
**WHERE TO LOOK** Bare acidic and clayey soils
**DESCRIPTION** Very similar to Clay Earth-moss (see above), but with much finer and longer (3–4mm), tapering leaves, which look like hair-points; the most distinctive feature is the abundant spherical, pale yellow-green capsules held on a very short seta, appearing as if growing from the ground
**SIMILAR SPECIES Clay Earth-moss** (see above); **Awl-leaved Earth-moss** *Pleuridium subulatum* is difficult to separate without a hand lens and is normally found on less acidic soil

Detail of leaves and capsules

3mm

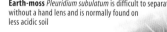

5mm

# Redshank
## *Ceratodon purpureus*

**HABITAT** Heathland, acid grassland and man-made structures
**WHERE TO LOOK** A very common moss found in a variety of
   situations including, gravelly paths, burnt areas, walls, roofs
   and on open soils in heathland and acid grassland
**DESCRIPTION** A variable moss (1–3cm tall), green-yellow to red-
   brown in colour, forming mats or cushions; leaves short (1.5–
   2mm), narrow and triangular with a wide nerve; upper leaves
   spread at an angle away from stem, lower leaves pressed
   against stem; leaves shrivelled and wavy when dry; dense mats
   of green capsules on a purple-red seta are common
**SIMILAR SPECIES** Unlikely to be confused
   with other species when
   capsules are present

15mm

Detail of leaves

26

# Common Pincushion
## *Dicranoweisia cirrata*

**HABITAT** Broadleaved woodland and rocky areas
**WHERE TO LOOK** A common moss found on the trunks and larger
   branches of ash, beech, oak and willow; also found on decaying
   wood, thatching and exposed rocks and stones
**DESCRIPTION** Small to medium-sized moss (2–3cm) forming thick,
   light green to yellow-green cushions; leaves narrow and wavy
   (2.5mm long), leaf margins also wavy, giving cushions a ragged
   look; when dry, leaves crunch up in a tight, curly mass; capsules
   common, brown on a yellow seta, protruding from cushion of
   leaves like pins in a pincushion
**SIMILAR SPECIES** **Mountain Fork-moss** *Dicranum
   montanum*, rare but increasing,
   is found on tree boles
   and dead wood

Detail of dry leaves

8mm

# Variable Forklet-moss
## *Dicranella varia*

**HABITAT** Quarries, paths and cuttings, grassland and arable land
**WHERE TO LOOK** Found in open areas such as paths, gravelly roads and quarries on calcareous soils; also found in open areas of calcareous grassland and arable land
**DESCRIPTION** Very small moss forming green to green-brown open patches; leaves small (2mm long) and narrow, often erect or all curved to one side; distinctive red-purple capsules on a red seta are common; calyptra claw-like
**SIMILAR SPECIES** **Field Forklet-moss** *Dicranella staphylina*, a common moss of arable land, has slightly translucent leaves which rarely curve to one side and does not have capsules

Detail of capsules

3mm

6mm

# Silky Forklet-moss
## *Dicranella heteromalla*

**HABITAT** Acid woodland, conifer plantations and heathland
**WHERE TO LOOK** Common moss found on banks, tree roots and stumps in acidic habitats
**DESCRIPTION** A bright green moss (2–3cm tall) forming cushions, patches or wefts; leaves, wisped over in one direction, are narrow and hair-like (3–3.5mm long), with teeth present near tip, leaf base wider and egg-shaped (both features seen through a hand lens); brown capsules (erect or drooping) on a yellow-brown seta are common; calyptra claw-like
**SIMILAR SPECIES** **Cape Thread-moss** *Orthodontium lineare* (see p.45)

Detail of leaves and capsules

2mm

4mm

# Broom Fork-moss
*Dicranum scoparium*

**HABITAT** Broadleaved woodlands and heathland
**WHERE TO LOOK** On the ground forming dense patches and
    hummocks, sometimes as cushions on trunks and branches
**DESCRIPTION** Medium to large moss (2–10cm) with leaves yellow-
    green (4–8mm long), narrow, tapering to a point and often
    sickle-shaped; minute teeth are visible along the leaf tip with a
    hand lens; long, dark green leaves spiral along the main stem;
    fruiting capsules (uncommon) 5–6 angled; seta up to 7–8cm
**SIMILAR SPECIES** **Greater Fork-moss** (see below); **Fragile Fork-
    moss** *Dicranum tauricum* found on stumps and logs
    often has broken leaf tips; **Crisped Fork-
    moss** *Dicranum bonjeanii* found
    in wet grassland is larger
    and has wavy leaves

15mm

Detail of leaves

# Greater Fork-moss
*Dicranum majus*

**HABITAT** Humid, acid woodland and conifer plantations
**WHERE TO LOOK** An uncommon moss found mainly with
    immature birch and in conifer plantations in Berks, and in
    Chiltern beechwoods
**DESCRIPTION** A large moss (to 12cm tall) forming large, looser
    patches than Broom Fork-moss (see above); leaves (10–14mm
    long) taper to a long, fine tip and all strongly curved in the
    same direction; capsules on a yellow seta, sometimes with
    several capsules produced from a single shoot.
**SIMILAR SPECIES** **Broom Fork-moss** (see above)
    has smaller, less curved leaves

15mm

Detail of leaves

# Dwarf Swan-neck Moss
*Campylopus pyriformis*

**HABITAT** Acid woodland, conifer plantations and heathland
**WHERE TO LOOK** Found on sandy and peaty acid soils and with gorse in the Chilterns; also found on tree stumps and tree bases
**DESCRIPTION** Messy moss forming a yellow-green blanket (1–3cm tall), often littered with broken leaves and shoots; leaves (2–7mm long) very narrow, straight and hair-like, wider at the base; wide nerve (seen through a hand lens); leaves and shoot tips fragile and easily removed; capsules occasional, similar to Heath Star-moss (see below)
**SIMILAR SPECIES Rusty Swan-neck Moss**
*Campylopus flexuosus* forms dark green patches; leaves and shoots do not break away

Detail of deciduous leaves

6mm

12mm

# Heath Star-moss
*Campylopus introflexus*

**HABITAT** Bare peat, conifer plantations and heathland
**WHERE TO LOOK** Burnt heath, peaty soil and conifer litter, also found on fence posts and tree stumps
**DESCRIPTION** Distinctive moss, forming dark green-black patches (2–5cm tall); leaves (2–6mm) with a translucent white nerve (often bent) that protrudes from the leaf tip up to two-thirds length of leaf; when dry, the leaves close up and the white leaf points flick outward, appearing star-shaped (giving the species its name); capsules frequent, often buried into the moss patch on looping, down-curved seta
**SIMILAR SPECIES** Unlikely to be confused with other species

Detail of eaves

5mm

8mm

# Large White-moss
## *Leucobryum glaucum*

**HABITAT** Acid woodland, conifer plantations and heathland
**WHERE TO LOOK** Found on the woodland floor on acidic soils under beech, oak and conifers, also found on wet heaths and bogs; found in abundance on some sites in Berks and the Chilterns
**DESCRIPTION** A large (2–10cm tall), glaucous-green moss (whitish when dry), forming extensive, dense cushions and hummocks, which, when dry, can become detached from the soil and be blown around like tumbleweed; leaves (6–9mm long) thick, hair-like, often rigid and straight, overlap tightly when dry
**SIMILAR SPECIES Smaller White-moss** *Leucobryum juniperoideum* has shorter leaves and forms shallower hummocks

Detail of leaves

15mm

# Narrow-leaved Pocket-moss
## *Fissidens gracilifolius*

**HABITAT** Woodland on limestone
**WHERE TO LOOK** Infrequent moss found on limestone fragments in deep shade of woodland in north and west Oxfordshire
**DESCRIPTION** A minute, patch-forming pocket-moss (to 5mm tall) with leaves arranged in an even, flat plane along the stem; each leaf has a smaller leaf overlapping below (creating a 'pocket'); individual leaves long and tongue-shaped (0.5–1.5mm), drawing to a point, with longer leaves near the top of the shoot
**SIMILAR SPECIES Petty Pocket-moss** *Fissidens pusillus,* very rare, is difficult to separate from Narrow-leaved Pocket-moss; **Green Pocket-moss** *Fissidens viridulus* does not grow on rock and has nipple-like tip to the leaf

Detail of leaves

4mm

# Common Pocket-moss
*Fissidens taxifolius*

**HABITAT** Woodland, hedgerows, grassland and arable fields
**WHERE TO LOOK** A common pocket-moss found in damp and
shady areas of banks, ditches and paths on clay and chalk soils;
also found in open soil on grassland and stubble fields
**DESCRIPTION** Medium-sized moss (to 2cm); leaf arrangement as
Narrow-leaved Pocket-moss; leaves long, tongue-shaped and
borderless, getting shorter towards tip of shoot; nerve runs to
tip of leaf (seen through a hand lens); capsules frequent on a
red seta (which bends near the base of capsule)
**SIMILAR SPECIES Lesser Pocket-moss** *Fissidens bryoides*
has erect capsules and **Short-leaved
Pocket-moss** *Fissidens incurvus*
has inclined capsules, both
have bordered leaves

Capsules

5mm

6mm

31

# Maidenhair Pocket-moss
*Fissidens adianthoides*

**HABITAT** Chalk grassland and fens
**WHERE TO LOOK** Found on shorter chalk grasslands and calcareous
fens, also found in wet heath areas on Greenham Common
**DESCRIPTION** A large pocket-moss (up to 5cm tall) of a distinctive
bright green colour; leaf arrangement as Narrow-leaved
Pocket-moss; leaves borderless with widely spaced teeth (seen
through a hand lens) fan out at tip of each shoot, with central
leaf longer than those on either side; capsules frequent, often
growing from halfway up the plant shoot (a notable feature)
**SIMILAR SPECIES Rock Pocket-moss** *Fissidens dubius*,
found on calcareous grassland, is difficult
to separate from Maidenhair
Pocket-moss without a
microscope

Capsules

5mm

5mm

# Crisp Beardless-moss
*Weissia longifolia* var. *angustifolia*

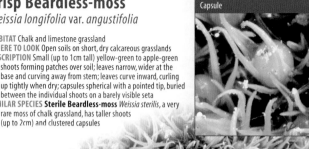

Capsule

**HABITAT** Chalk and limestone grassland
**WHERE TO LOOK** Open soils on short, dry calcareous grasslands
**DESCRIPTION** Small (up to 1cm tall) yellow-green to apple-green
shoots forming patches over soil; leaves narrow, wider at the
base and curving away from stem; leaves curve inward, curling
up tightly when dry; capsules spherical with a pointed tip, buried
between the individual shoots on a barely visible seta
**SIMILAR SPECIES Sterile Beardless-moss** *Weissia sterilis*, a very
rare moss of chalk grassland, has taller shoots
(up to 2cm) and clustered capsules

4mm

# Curly Crisp-moss
*Trichostomum crispulum*

Detail of leaves: wet (LEFT), dry (RIGHT)

**HABITAT** Grassland
**WHERE TO LOOK** A rare moss of chalk grassland, also found on
gravelly ground near heath on Greenham Common
**DESCRIPTION** Small, bright yellow-green to deep green moss
(often more brown near the leaf base), forming tight blankets
and patches; leaves (2–2.5mm long) with rounded edges and a
hooded leaf tip (seen through a hand lens) have a wavy
appearance; leaves curl up tightly when dry and look like dead
spider legs
**SIMILAR SPECIES** Unlikely to be confused with
other species

4mm

# Revolute Beard-moss
*Pseudocrossidium revolutum*

Detail of leaves

1.5mm

**HABITAT** Man-made structures, quarries and rocky outcrops
**WHERE TO LOOK** Found on mortar on top of walls, on limestone
walls, slabs and chippings, and on limestone in quarries
**DESCRIPTION** Tiny bright green moss forming cushions and turfs;
leaves (1.5mm long) with strongly inrolled edges that look like
rolled-up scrolls along the sides of the leaf (seen through a hand
lens), blunt tipped with nerve creating a very thin and short
point; leaves are erect or spreading from the stem when moist
and curl up tightly when dry; capsules are occasionally present
**SIMILAR SPECIES Hornschuch's Beard-moss**
*Pseudocrossidium hornschuchianum*
is very similar, but has
sharp-pointed leaves

3mm

# Pointed Lattice-moss
*Dialytrichia mucronata*

Detail of leaves

2mm

**HABITAT** Flood zone of rivers and streams
**WHERE TO LOOK** Beside rivers and streams where flooding occurs
on silted soils, rocks and concrete, tree bases and decaying wood
**DESCRIPTION** Small, dark green moss (2–4mm tall) with green-
black leaves further down the stem; leaves (2–3.5mm long)
have thickened margins and are tongue-shaped with a rounded
tip and protruding nerve; when dry plants twist up and appear
paler in colour
**SIMILAR SPECIES Water Screw-moss** *Syntrichia latifolia*
(see p.40) has larger leaves, widest near
the tip, with the leaf nerve
not protruding

6mm

# Bird's-claw Beard-moss
*Barbula unguiculata*

Detail of leaves

**HABITAT** Disturbed and open habitats and man-made structures
**WHERE TO LOOK** Found on disturbed calcareous soils, clay, sand and gravel, on walls, in gardens and in quarries
**DESCRIPTION** Medium-sized moss (up to 1.5cm tall) growing in bright yellow-green patches; leaves (1.5–2mm long) tongue-shaped with a protruding nerve, fold inwards for much of their length; leaves spread away from the stem when moist, but twist up when dry; capsules occasional, on an erect, red seta
**SIMILAR SPECIES Lesser Bird's-claw Beard-moss** *Barbula convoluta*, a smaller, very common moss, has a sharper leaf with a short protruding nerve, capsules on a yellow seta

5mm

34

# Rigid Beard-moss
*Didymodon rigidulus*

Detail of leaves with attenuated tips

**HABITAT** Churchyards, man-made structures and quarries
**WHERE TO LOOK** Found on shaded limestone walls, concrete and stones in churchyards and on rock in limestone quarries
**DESCRIPTION** A small, dark green moss (0.5–1cm) often forming rounded tufts; leaves short and triangular (1.5–3mm long), tapering to a sharply pointed tip, nerve prominent; leaves close up when dry; capsules occasional
**SIMILAR SPECIES Dusky Beard-moss** *Didymodon luridus* has shorter, wider blunt-tipped leaves; **Soft-fruited Beard-moss** *Didymodon vinealis* is a paler green, has narrower, longer leaves and forms looser cushions; **Nicholson's Beard-moss** *Didymodon nicholsonii* has a wider leaf base and a keeled leaf tip

5mm

# Cylindric Beard-moss
*Didymodon insulanus*

**HABITAT** Man-made structures, disturbed habitats, quarries, wet woodland, and near rivers and streams
**WHERE TO LOOK** This common moss is found on open soil, but also grows on concrete, brick walls, tarmac and stone slabs, and on tree trunks and roots near rivers and streams
**DESCRIPTION** A distinctive rusty orange to olive green moss, forming extensive patches or open tufts (0.5–3cm tall); leaves long and very narrow (3–4mm long), curving in the same direction around the stem (in a spiral when viewed from above); when dry the leaves curl up tightly
**SIMILAR SPECIES** **False Beard-moss** *Didymodon fallax*, similar in colour, has much shorter, less curved, leaves

Detail of leaves

3mm

6mm

# Common Aloe-moss
*Aloina aloides*

**HABITAT** Quarries, man-made structures and calcareous grassland
**WHERE TO LOOK** An uncommon moss, found on loose, open calcareous soil and hard, stony ground in quarries and pits
**DESCRIPTION** A very small, dark green to brown-green moss (2–5mm tall) found in loose patches; leaves (3–4mm long) glossy, succulent and erect, forming a rosette (like miniature aloes), stiffening and becoming more aloe-like when dry; leaves appear thickened with sides folded inward, meeting at the leaf tip in a small hood (seen through a hand lens); capsules often abundant
**SIMILAR SPECIES** **Tall Aloe-moss** *Aloina ambigua* has a membrane between the capsule mouth and the teeth (seen through a hand lens); **Rigid Aloe-moss** *Aloina rigida* is much smaller

Detail of leaves

3mm

7mm

# Wall Screw-moss
*Tortula muralis*

Detail of leaves

**HABITAT** Man-made structures and rocks

**WHERE TO LOOK** One of the commonest mosses of urban areas; found on brick walls, limestone, concrete and roofing tiles, and on base-rich rock outcrops

**DESCRIPTION** Grows in small patches and cushions with short, tongue-shaped, green leaves (2–3.5mm) with a long translucent white hair point; capsules present through most of the year and held above the leaves on yellow-red seta; calyptra claw-like

**SIMILAR SPECIES** **Bordered Screw-moss** *Tortula marginata* lacks the long white hair points

6mm

# Common Pottia
*Tortula truncata*

Detail of capsule

**HABITAT** Arable fields, gardens, grasslands and woodland rides

**WHERE TO LOOK** Found on open acid soils, often where soil has been disturbed (e.g. hoof prints of livestock or in stubble fields)

**DESCRIPTION** Minute individual or clustered plants (2–5mm tall); leaves tongue-shaped (2mm long) with a central nerve; single cup-like capsules, widest at the rim, often present in the centre of individual plants on a yellow-brown seta; calyptra claw-like

**SIMILAR SPECIES** **Blunt-fruited Pottia** *Tortula modica* is taller (1.5cm) and has a similar-shaped capsule, longer than wide; **Lance-leaved Pottia** *Tortula lanceola* does not have a cup-shaped capsule

3mm

# Cuspidate Earth-moss
*Phascum cuspidatum*

**HABITAT** Arable fields, gardens, grasslands and woodland rides
**WHERE TO LOOK** Found on open soils, often where soil has been disturbed (e.g. hoof prints of livestock or in stubble fields)
**DESCRIPTION** Densely packed or individual, egg-shaped leafy plants (2–6mm tall); large leaves (1–3mm long), with a prominent leaf tip pointing inward, surround capsule; capsules egg-shaped and orange-green; seta not visible
**SIMILAR SPECIES Rounded Pygmy-moss** *Acaulon muticum* is very similar, but is a much rarer moss found on more acid soils, and has fewer leaves surrounding each capsule

Detail of leaves and capsules

2mm

4mm

# Upright Pottia
*Microbryum rectum*

**HABITAT** Arable fields, grasslands and quarries
**WHERE TO LOOK** Found on open calcareous soils, often where soil has been disturbed (e.g. hoof prints of livestock or in stubble fields)
**DESCRIPTION** One of the smallest mosses found on disturbed soils (less than 1mm tall), found as individual plants or in open patches; leaves less than 1mm long with a spear shaped tip and curved inwards (along the nerve); distinctive spherical capsule on top of an upright, short seta (0.6–1mm tall); calyptra claw-like
**SIMILAR SPECIES Swan-necked Earth-moss** *Microbryum curvicollum* is a similar size, but has drooping capsules

Detail of leaves and capsules

1mm

2mm

# Sand-hill Screw-moss
*Syntrichia ruralis* var. *ruraliformis*

**HABITAT** Man-made structures and roads, sandy soils, quarries
**WHERE TO LOOK** Often found on concrete and asbestos roofing, also found on sand deposits in quarries
**DESCRIPTION** Golden green to orange brown clustered moss; leaves (4–6mm long) gradually taper into the leaf tip with a white hair-point, when moist the leaves curve back strongly, when dry they screw up tightly and appear a much darker green-brown
**SIMILAR SPECIES** **Great Hairy Screw-moss** *Syntrichia ruralis* var. *ruralis* found on walls, rocks and sandy ground, but leaves finish bluntly and do not taper into the white hair-point; **Intermediate Screw-moss** (see below)

Detail of leaves

12mm

38

# Intermediate Screw-moss
*Syntrichia montana*

**HABITAT** Man-made structures and rocks
**WHERE TO LOOK** Often found in calcareous places, such as roofs, limestone walls, rocks and stony ground
**DESCRIPTION** Golden-green clustered plants, forming small cushions (1–4cm tall); leaves (4mm long), with strong red nerve, finish bluntly before a long, translucent white hair-point; when moist the leaves spread out, when dry they twist up, appearing a much darker grey-green; capsules are often present on a red seta
**SIMILAR SPECIES** **Great Hairy Screw-moss** *Syntrichia ruralis* var. *ruralis* rarely produces capsules

Detail of leaves

8mm

# Small Hairy Screw-moss
*Syntrichia laevipila*

Capsules

7mm

**HABITAT** Broadleaved woodlands and hedgerows
**WHERE TO LOOK** Found on the branches of elder, ash and willow
**DESCRIPTION** Bright green patches of rosette-forming plants (1–1.5cm tall). Leaves (2.5–3.5mm) bluntly rounded with a long, translucent hair-point; leaves spread out when moist and twist up tightly when dry; capsules are common
**SIMILAR SPECIES Lesser Screw-moss** *Syntrichia virescens*, a much rarer moss, has distinctive teeth along the hair-point and a lightly notched leaf tip

2.5mm

# Marble Screw-moss
*Syntrichia papillosa*

Detail of wet leaves with gemmae

2mm

**HABITAT** Broadleaved woodlands, hedgerows and solitary trees
**WHERE TO LOOK** A uncommon moss that appears to be spreading, found on mature ash, willow and elder
**DESCRIPTION** Small, dark green patches (2–10mm tall); leaves (2.5mm long) spread out when moist and twist up tightly when dry; leaf margins curve in strongly, towards the nerve which protrudes from the leaf tip; the distinguishing feature of this moss is the collection of green orb-like gemmae that collect along the central nerve and leaf tip
**SIMILAR SPECIES** Unlikely to be confused with other species

3mm

# Water Screw-moss
*Syntrichia latifolia*

**HABITAT** Flood zone of rivers and streams
**WHERE TO LOOK** Beside rivers and streams where flooding occurs, growing on tree bases and decaying wood, rocks and walls
**DESCRIPTION** Medium-sized, yellow-green to dark green moss (1–3cm tall), growing as loose or more compact patches, often heavily encrusted with silt; leaves broad (3mm long), tongue-shaped and spreading like a small flower, becoming shrivelled when dry; surface of leaves can be dotted with fine granular gemmae (seen through a hand lens)
**SIMILAR SPECIES Pointed Lattice-moss** *Dialytrichia mucronata* (see p.33), found in the same areas, has narrower, oval leaves

6mm

Detail of leaves

# Thickpoint Grimmia
*Schistidium crassipilum*

**HABITAT** Quarries, rocks and man-made structures
**WHERE TO LOOK** Found on calcareous rock, walls, concrete and brick. It can also be found on exposed chalk banks
**DESCRIPTION** Medium-sized, yellow-green to dark green moss (1–3cm tall), forming raised, circular cushions and flat patches; leaves narrow (1.5–2.5mm long), terminating in a white hair-point, giving the moss a spiky appearance, leaves turn blackish-green and close up when dry; distinctive red capsules abundant, surrounded by pointed, narrow leaves
**SIMILAR SPECIES Anomalous Bristle-moss** *Orthotrichum anomalum* (see p.54) growing in similar habitats, can appear similar but has capsules on a short seta

6mm

Detail of dry leaves and capsules

# Grey-cushioned Grimmia
*Grimmia pulvinata*

Detail of capsules

3mm

**HABITAT** Man-made structures, quarries and rocky outcrops
**WHERE TO LOOK** A very common urban moss found on walls, roofs, gravestones and tarmac
**DESCRIPTION** Medium-sized, hairy, grey-looking moss, forming raised, rounded cushions (1–2cm high); leaves with long, white hair points (sometimes shorter) at the tip (hair points more prominent than the darker, green leaves); capsules abundant on a curved seta, almost buried within the cushion (old capsules with a straight seta), bright green, oval, with a beaked lid
**SIMILAR SPECIES Round-fruited Grimmia**
*Grimmia orbicularis* with a nipple-like capsule lid, has been found on a few limestone walls in the past

6mm

# Woolly Fringe-moss
*Racomitrium lanuginosum*

Detail of leaves

6mm

**HABITAT** Rocky outcrops and man-made structures
**WHERE TO LOOK** Found mainly in the uplands of the north and west of Britain, it is a rare moss in our region, found on stone and slag in a few disused railway cuttings, such as Hook Norton Cutting Nature Reserve in north Oxfordshire
**DESCRIPTION** Large, bushy and distinctive grey-green moss (to several cm long) with short branches; leaves (3–6cm long) with long, toothed hair points (seen through a hand lens); hair points can bend in one direction or be wavy and bend back away from the shoots in all directions
**SIMILAR SPECIES** Unlikely to be confused with other species

12mm

# Dwarf Rock-bristle
## *Seligeria pusilla*

**HABITAT** Woodland on limestone
**WHERE TO LOOK** Found on shaded oolitic limestone and
fragments, often on overhangs, in woodland in west
Oxfordshire, particularly those above the River Evenlode
**DESCRIPTION** A minute, dark green moss (2–3mm tall) growing in
mats of fine hair-like shoots; leaves minute (1mm), spearhead-
shaped and sharply pointed, with longer, narrower leaves
found around the base of seta. Capsules (uncommon, but can
be abundant) oval, on a short (2–3mm long), straight seta;
calyptra claw-like
**SIMILAR SPECIES English Rock-bristle**
(see below) is found mainly in
the Chilterns on chalk

Detail of leaves and capsules

4mm

# English Rock-bristle
## *Seligeria calycina*

**HABITAT** Woodland on chalk, chalk quarries
**WHERE TO LOOK** Found on chalk fragments in woodland and chalk
pits, mainly in the Chilterns.
**DESCRIPTION** A minute, olive-green to brown moss (2mm tall)
growing in mats of fine hair-like shoots; leaves minute (1mm
long), spearhead-shaped and sharply pointed), all of a similar
length; capsules common, elongated egg-shaped, on a short
(2.5–3mm long), straight seta; calyptra claw-like
**SIMILAR SPECIES Dwarf Rock-bristle** (see above); **Chalk Rock-
bristle** *Seligeria calcarea*, rare, on faces
of chalk in quarries, has a shorter
capsule and leaves with
a blunt point

Detail of dry leaves and capsules

4mm

# Common Extinguisher-moss
## *Encalypta vulgaris*

Detail of leaves

2mm

**HABITAT** Quarries and man-made structures
**WHERE TO LOOK** A uncommon moss, found on limestone walls and on earth-capped limestone rock in quarries
**DESCRIPTION** A medium-sized, light-green moss (1.5cm tall), forming open patches and clusters; leaves (3mm long) broadly tongue-shaped, pointed; capsules on a red-brown seta, abundant; calyptra distinctive, large and hooded (looking like an old-fashioned candle extinguisher) covering the capsule completely
**SIMILAR SPECIES** Unlikely to be confused with other species

6mm

# Spiral Extinguisher-moss
## *Encalypta streptocarpa*

Leaves with propagules in leaf axils

4mm

**HABITAT** Beech woodland, calcareous grassland, rocky outcrops and man-made structures
**WHERE TO LOOK** A local moss, found on calcareous soils in grassland, on beech roots in woodland, and on limestone walls
**DESCRIPTION** Large, dull, pale green moss (1–2cm tall) with leaves forming a loose 'floret'; leaves (4–7mm long) matt and opaque, wavy, parallel-sided and narrowing to a blunt tip; brown propagules often grow between the leaves and look like fine brown hairs; capsules are rarely present
**SIMILAR SPECIES** Unlikely to be confused with other species

5mm

# Bonfire-moss
*Funaria hygrometrica*

**HABITAT** Disturbed habitats
**WHERE TO LOOK** This common moss colonises disturbed ground and is often found on old bonfire sites
**DESCRIPTION** Green to brownish-green moss forming mats or open patches (shoots 3–10cm high); leaves translucent (2–4mm long), wide and oval drawing to a point; capsules abundant, large and green (when ripe) on a long and thin, swan-necked, brown-green seta; calyptra long-pointed, inflated
**SIMILAR SPECIES** Unlikely to be confused with other species when capsules are present

Wet leaves and capsules

6mm

# Common Bladder-moss
*Physcomitrium pyriforme*

**HABITAT** Disturbed habitats, arable fields and pastures
**WHERE TO LOOK** Found on open, recently disturbed, damp soils, especially on damp clods of earth in livestock-grazed pastures
**DESCRIPTION** Small green moss (5mm tall), growing as scattered plants or in loose clusters; leaves large (3–4mm long), egg-shaped, with a short, pointed tip; capsules common, large and pear-shaped with a pointed lid, on an erect seta; calyptra with long point
**SIMILAR SPECIES** **Hasselquist's Hyssop** *Entosthodon fascicularis* is similar, but is found on drier soils and does not have a pointed capsule lid

Detail of leaves and capsules

5mm

# Cape Thread-moss
*Orthodontium lineare*

**HABITAT** Acid woodland
**WHERE TO LOOK** Found on woodland banks, and on the sides of
logs, decaying wood and birch, beech and oak stumps
**DESCRIPTION** A fine, dark-green to olive-green moss (up to 1cm
tall) forming large patches and blankets; leaves very fine and
hair-like (up to 3mm long), becoming wavy when dry; capsules
common, pale green (mature capsules become red and
furrowed), gradually tapering to the curved, often drooping
seta; calyptra claw-like
**SIMILAR SPECIES Silky Forklet-moss** *Dicranella
heteromalla* (see p.27) with leaves
often turned in one direction,
has brown capsules

Detail of dry leaves and capsules

5mm

8mm

45

# Capillary Thread-moss
*Bryum capillare*

**HABITAT** Woodland, grassland and man-made structures
**WHERE TO LOOK** A very common moss growing on tree trunks and
branches, decaying wood, walls and on soil in grassland
**DESCRIPTION** Medium-sized moss with leaves forming a rounded
'floret' (in a tight spiral when dry), growing in tufts or patches
(1–3cm tall); leaves broad (2–5mm long), widest nearer tip,
with a whitish hair-point; capsules nodding, on a long, red seta
**SIMILAR SPECIES Nodding Thread-moss** *Pohlia nutans* (see
p.48), found on acid soils, also has nodding capsules; **Syed's
Thread-moss** *Bryum moravicum*, found on
tree trunks, has brown hair-like
gemmae between the leaves
and does not have
capsules

Detail of leaves

3mm

8mm

# Marsh Bryum
*Bryum pseudotriquetrum*

Capsules

**HABITAT** Wetland, wet heathland, marshes and fen
**WHERE TO LOOK** Found at edges of lakes and ponds, and wet heathland, marshes and fen; abundant at Greenham Common and Decoy Heath in Berks
**DESCRIPTION** A large and erect, green to brownish, sometimes reddish, moss (7–10cm), forming patches and cushions; leaves (2–3.5mm long) with strong, red nerve finishing in a small point, equally spaced on a prominent red stem; lower part of the plant is covered in brown hairs; male plants with a 'flower' of leaves at the shoot tips; capsules large and pendulous, on a long seta
**SIMILAR SPECIES** Unlikely to be confused with other species

6mm

# Bicoloured Bryum
*Bryum dichotomum*

Detail of leaves with bulbils

**HABITAT** Disturbed habitats, arable land, man-made structures, urban areas, gardens and quarries
**WHERE TO LOOK** A common moss found on open soil in recently disturbed habitats such as tracks and paths, also grows on thin layers of soil collected on top of walls and rocks
**DESCRIPTION** Small, green moss appearing in small patches of tightly clustered shoots (up to 1cm tall); leaves short and wide (2–2.5mm long) with a tapered tip; green bulbils (between 1–5) collect in leaf axils (seen through a hand lens); capsules drooping, in reds, yellows and greens, on a red to yellow seta
**SIMILAR SPECIES** **Small-bud Bryum** *Bryum gemmiferum* has more bulbils (20–30) in leaf axils

6mm

# Silver-moss
*Bryum argenteum*

**Capsules**

2mm

**HABITAT** Disturbed habitats, man-made structures, urban areas, gardens and quarries
**WHERE TO LOOK** A very common moss of urban areas, found on open soil in recently disturbed habitats such as tracks and paths; also grows on rock, stone, tarmac, brick and concrete
**DESCRIPTION** Small, green moss with silvery-white tips forming patches of tightly clustered shoots (up to 1cm tall); leaves minute (0.75–1.25mm long), egg-shaped, overlapping and pressed to the stem; capsules drooping, in a variety of browns, reds and greens, on a short seta
**SIMILAR SPECIES** Green forms can look like **Bicoloured Bryum** *Bryum dichotomum* (see p.46)

4mm

# Rose-moss
*Rhodobryum roseum*

**Detail of leaves**

4mm

**HABITAT** Chalk and limestone grassland
**WHERE TO LOOK** A rare moss of calcareous grassland, favouring the large anthills of the Yellow Meadow Ant, such as those found at Aston Rowant National Nature Reserve in the Chilterns
**DESCRIPTION** A distinctive, yellow-green moss, forming large rosettes of leaves (10–12mm across) at the top of secondary branches from a creeping main stem; leaves large (4.5–mm long), spear-shaped with a jagged tip, softly wavy and curved inwards to halfway along the length
**SIMILAR SPECIES** Unlikely to be confused with other species

5mm

# Nodding Thread-moss
## *Pohlia nutans*

Detail of leaves

**HABITAT** Woodland, heathland and grassland
**WHERE TO LOOK** A common moss found on acid soils in woodland
and on open soil in heathland and acid grassland
**DESCRIPTION** A medium-sized, green to brownish-green moss
(1–2cm tall); leaves spear-shaped (2.5–4.5mm long) and
clustered towards the tip of the shoots; capsules abundant,
nodding, on a long, red seta.
**SIMILAR SPECIES Capillary Thread-moss** *Bryum capillare*
(see p.46), prefers less acid soils and also has nodding
capsules on a red seta

10mm

# Swan's-neck Thyme-moss
## *Mnium hornum*

Capsules

**HABITAT** Acid woodland
**WHERE TO LOOK** A very common moss of acidic soils in woodland,
on tree stumps and among tree roots
**DESCRIPTION** A large, dark green moss with erect or drooping
shoots (2–4cm tall); leaves large (3–8mm long), oval, with a
toothed border (seen through a hand lens); leaves are much
smaller and triangular, further down the stem; male plants
often form a distinctive green 'floret' with a brown centre;
capsules common, drooping, on long seta (2–5cm long)
**SIMILAR SPECIES Starry Thyme-moss** *Mnium
stellare*, an uncommon moss found
mainly in the Chilterns, is
paler and has more
rounded leaves

15mm

# Dotted Thyme-moss
*Rhizomnium punctatum*

Male plants

4mm

**HABITAT** Wet woodland, fens and marshes
**WHERE TO LOOK** Found on wet soils, decaying wood and tree
bases in woodland, and in fens and marshes
**DESCRIPTION** A distinctive, medium to large, green to brownish-
green moss (1–10cm tall), with shoots and leaf axils matted
with fine brown hairs; leaves large (5–6mm long), broad and
egg-shaped, translucent and bordered, with a prominent nerve;
male plants have a characteristic leafy 'floret' with a dark brown
centre, at the tip of the shoot; capsules not common
**SIMILAR SPECIES Felted Thyme-moss** *Rhizomnium*
*pseudopunctatum* is a rare moss
found in fens in the Cothill
area of Oxfordshire

6mm

# Hart's-tongue Thyme-moss
*Plagiomnium undulatum*

Detail of leaves

3mm

**HABITAT** Wet woodland and wet grassland
**WHERE TO LOOK** A common moss of wet clay and calcareous soils,
pathways and stream banks in woodland, and in wet grassland
**DESCRIPTION** A large, pale yellow-green moss, with shoots (up to
15cm long) varying in form – appearing long with distant
leaves or as shorter shoots with leaves growing like a palm tree;
leaves long and characteristically undulating (2–5mm long),
tongue-shaped with toothed border, slightly translucent;
capsules uncommon
**SIMILAR SPECIES** Unlikely to be confused with
other species, but young shoots
can look similar to other
*Plagiomnium* species

12mm

# Woodsy Thyme-moss
*Plagiomnium cuspidatum*

**HABITAT** Humid woodland
**WHERE TO LOOK** A rare moss of humid woodland on calcareous soils and rocks, often near water
**DESCRIPTION** Medium-sized moss (1.5–4cm tall), with trailing shoots of widely spaced, pale green leaves; leaves (1.5–3.5mm long) rounded, tapering to a sharp point, with a prominent nerve that protrudes; upper leaf edge is sharply toothed (seen through a hand lens) and the lower edge is smooth; capsules are rare in our region
**SIMILAR SPECIES Many-fruited Thyme-moss** *Plagiomnium affine* has oval leaves with the entire leaf edge toothed

Detail of leaves

5mm

# Long-beaked Thyme-moss
*Plagiomnium rostratum*

**HABITAT** Calcareous woodland, quarries and fens
**WHERE TO LOOK** Found on hard calcareous soils in woodland, bases of walls, in old quarries and fens
**DESCRIPTION** A medium-sized, green to dark green moss, with creeping shoots (up to 5cm long); leaves round to oval (5–7mm long), with a plain border, do not run onto the stem; capsules with a beaked lid
**SIMILAR SPECIES Tall Thyme-moss** *Plagiomnium elatum*, larger with erect shoots and **Marsh Thyme-moss** *Plagiomnium ellipticum* are both found in wet habitats; **Many-fruited Thyme-moss** *Plagiomnium affine* has toothed leaves

Detail of capsule

10mm

# Bog Bead-moss
*Aulacomnium palustre*

Male plants

**HABITAT** Bogs and wet heathland
**WHERE TO LOOK** A locally common moss of valley bogs and wet heathland in Berks (often associated with *Sphagnum* mosses)
**DESCRIPTION** A large, bushy moss, forming tufts (3–12cm tall) with pale yellow-green leaves and a mat of brown-ginger, thread-like hairs along the main stem; shoot tips of male plants sometimes have a cluster of brown gemmae (see right); leaves (4–6mm long) triangular and narrow with a small pointed tip
**SIMILAR SPECIES** Unlikely to be confused with other species

# Drumsticks
*Aulacomnium androgynum*

Balls of gemmae on stalks

**HABITAT** Humid woodland
**WHERE TO LOOK** Found in woodland on peaty banks, decaying wood and bases of trees, also as an epiphyte on elder and willow in wet woodland
**DESCRIPTION** A small, pale green moss, forming small tufts and cushions (3–4mm tall); overlapping leaves (1–2mm long) triangular and narrow, with a small pointed tip; distinctive feature of the moss is the ball of gemmae held on a thick stalk above the cushion of leaves (looking like miniature drumsticks
**SIMILAR SPECIES** Unlikely to be confused with other species

# Green Yoke-moss
*Zygodon viridissimus*

**HABITAT** Woodland
**WHERE TO LOOK** An epiphytic moss growing on the trunks of ash, elder, field maple, sycamore and willow
**DESCRIPTION** Small, bright green moss (to 1cm tall) forming open or dense patches; leaves narrow and long (1.5–2mm long), curving inwards along the length; leaves spread out when wet and crunch up, with the stems curving upwards, when dry
**SIMILAR SPECIES** **Lesser Yoke-moss** *Zygodon conoideus* often produces capsules and has shorter, straighter leaves; the rarer **Park Yoke-moss** *Zygodon rupestris* prefers old oak and ash, and is more yellow-green in colour

Detail of dry leaves

10mm

# Wood Bristle-moss
*Orthotrichum affine*

**HABITAT** Woodland
**WHERE TO LOOK** A common epiphytic moss growing on branches and trunks of elder, willow, ash, sycamore, hazel and young oak
**DESCRIPTION** Medium-sized moss forming clumps and tufts (0.8–3.5cm tall); leaves narrow (3mm long), margins curving inwards; capsules abundant within the shoots (no seta visible), long and cylindrical (heavily furrowed when dry) with 8 star-like outer teeth; calyptra slightly hairy
**SIMILAR SPECIES** The rare **Smooth Bristle-moss** *Orthotrichum striatum*, has capsules smooth when dry, with 16 inner and 16 outer teeth; **Slender Bristle-moss** *Orthotrichum tenellum* is smaller with narrower capsules and a long calyptra

Detail of wet leaves and capsules

5mm

# Lyell's Bristle-moss
*Orthotrichum lyellii*

**HABITAT** Woodland

**WHERE TO LOOK** An uncommon epiphytic moss growing on the branches and trunks of ash, poplar, sycamore, elder, willow and young oak

**DESCRIPTION** Large, bushy green moss (3–4cm tall), often sprawling and drooping from trunks and branches with long individual shoots; leaves narrow (3.5mm long), drawing to a sharp point; leaves and stems covered in fine, ginger-brown, granular gemmae (the number of gemmae often make the lower parts of the plant appear brown in colour)

**SIMILAR SPECIES** Unlikely to be confused with other species

Detail of leaves with gemmae

4mm

3mm

# Elegant Bristle-moss
*Orthotrichum pulchellum*

**HABITAT** Humid woodland and willow carr

**WHERE TO LOOK** An uncommon (apparently spreading) epiphytic moss growing on branches and trunks of willow and elder

**DESCRIPTION** A medium-sized (0.5–2cm tall) yellow-green moss forming clumps and patches; leaves (2–2.5mm long) narrow, tapering to a point, twisted when dry; capsules held above leaves on a short seta, orange teeth at capsule mouth; calyptra pointed, pale with dark brown dots at the base

**SIMILAR SPECIES** The rare **Straw Bristle-moss** *Orthotrichum stramineum* forms neat cushions, with capsules held just clear of leaves on a short seta, calyptra with red-brown tip

Dry leaves and old capsules

2.5mm

4mm

# White-tipped Bristle-moss
*Orthotrichum diaphanum*

Detail of dry leaves and capsules

**HABITAT** Woodland and man-made structures
**WHERE TO LOOK** An epiphytic moss found on branches and trunks of willow and especially on elder, sometimes found on concrete and brick walls
**DESCRIPTION** This distinctive Bristle-moss forms small green cushions (up to 1cm tall) and is the only Bristle-moss whose leaves (2.5–4mm long) have long, white hair-tips; capsules common, brown and furrowed when dry; capsule mouth with 16 widely spreading, light brown, outer teeth; calyptra light green, hairless
**SIMILAR SPECIES** Unlikely to be confused with other species

4mm

# Anomalous Bristle-moss
*Orthotrichum anomalum*

Detail of dry leaves and capsules

**HABITAT** Quarries, rocky outcrops and man-made structures
**WHERE TO LOOK** A common moss found on unshaded rocks, limestone walls, concrete and gravestones.
**DESCRIPTION** A medium-sized moss forming small cushions (1.5cm tall); leaves (2.5–4mm long) green when moist, but brown and appearing burnt when dry; capsules (green when unripe, red-brown when mature, strongly furrowed when dry), protrude well clear of the cushion on a short seta; calyptra hairy
**SIMILAR SPECIES** **Hooded Bristle-moss** *Orthotrichum cupulatum* (see p.55); **Thickpoint Grimmia** *Schistidium crassipilum* has red capsules, not protruding from the cushion

5mm

# Hooded Bristle-moss
*Orthotrichum cupulatum*

Dry leaves and capsules

6mm

**HABITAT** Man-made structures
**WHERE TO LOOK** An uncommon moss (often growing with Anomalous Bristle-moss), found on limestone walls and bridges near water, weirs and locks
**DESCRIPTION** This moss is very similar in appearance to Anomalous Bristle-moss but is only easily identifiable when abundant capsules are present in spring; leaves dark green (3.5–4mm long), blackish and pressed to stem when dry; capsules are held close to the plant on a barely visible seta (unlike the much taller seta of Anomalous Bristle-moss); calyptra hairless or with a few hairs
**SIMILAR SPECIES Anomalous Bristle-moss** *Orthotrichum anomalum* (see p.54)

3mm

# Crisped Pincushion
*Ulota crispa*

Damp leaves and capsules

2mm

**HABITAT** Woodland
**WHERE TO LOOK** An epiphyte found on ash, hazel, oak and willow
**DESCRIPTION** A bright yellow-green moss forming bushy, circular cushions (0.5–2cm tall); leaves narrow, long and triangular (2–3.5mm long), spreading when moist and tightly curled up when dry; capsules erect on a short seta protrude from the cushion (looking like a pincushion), furrowed and narrowing just before the mouth when old; calyptra with long hairs
**SIMILAR SPECIES Bruch's Pincushion** *Ulota bruchii* is very similar, but old capsules are more barrel-shaped, narrowing to a small mouth

3mm

# Frizzled Pincushion
*Ulota phyllantha*

**HABITAT** Humid woodland, carr and scrub
**WHERE TO LOOK** An epiphytic moss found on the branches and
trunks of willow, ash, birch, elder, hazel and oak
**DESCRIPTION** Medium-size moss (1–3.5cm tall) forming pale-
green cushions; leaves straight and narrow (2.5mm–4.5mm
long), curling up tightly when dry; does not produce capsules
but a cluster of small, light to dark brown, vegetative bulbils
(gemmae) are often found near the tip of the shoots
**SIMILAR SPECIES** Unlikely to be confused with other *Ulota* species
when gemmae are visible

Detail of wet leaves and gemmae

8mm

# Lateral Cryphaea
*Cryphaea heteromalla*

**HABITAT** Woodland and scrub
**WHERE TO LOOK** An epiphytic moss found on tree trunks,
especially elder, willow and ash
**DESCRIPTION** A distinctive medium-sized, dark green moss
(shoots 1.5cm long), with branches creeping tightly against
trunks and secondary branches held erect horizontally; leaves
(1–1.3mm long) spread slightly when wet and are held close to
the stem when dry; capsules distinctive, several together,
surrounded by narrow, tapering leaves, are held along one side
of the erect shoots, making the moss look
like a tiny heather plant
**SIMILAR SPECIES** Unlikely to be
confused with other species

Detail of capsules

5mm

# Tree-moss
## *Climacium dendroides*

**HABITAT** Wet woodland, fens, flushes, grassland and heathland
**WHERE TO LOOK** A rare moss of damp and wet areas with
fluctuating water levels
**DESCRIPTION** A large, distinctive tree-like, yellow-brown to
yellow-green moss (2–3 cm tall), secondary branches growing
from stem give the plant its tree-like appearance, plants can
also be quite stunted and branching in a cluster from near the
soil surface; leaves thick (2–3.5 long), sometimes translucent
and overlapping when dry and spreading when moist
**SIMILAR SPECIES Fox-tail Feather-moss**
*Thamnobryum alopecurum* (see p.58), a dark
green tree-like moss, is much
more common and is
found in woodland

Detail of leaves

10mm

20mm

57

# Flat Neckera
## *Neckera complanata*

**HABITAT** Woodland, hedgerows, limestone walls and rock
**WHERE TO LOOK** Growing on bases of ash and field maple, also on
limestone walls (often abundant) and rock
**DESCRIPTION** A fine-leaved, branching, green to silvery-green
moss (shoots to 5cm long), with shoots fanning out from
clumps, fine thread-like branches are also present weaved
through the main clump; leaves small (2mm long), concave and
rounded with a small nipple-like point, silvery, terminal leaves
of each shoot look like a small rounded helmet
**SIMILAR SPECIES Crisped Neckera** *Neckera crispa* and
**Dwarf Neckera** *Neckera pumila* have wavy
leaves; **Blunt Feather-moss**
*Homalia trichomanoides* (see
p.58) is a darker green

Detail of leaves

4mm

8mm

# Blunt Feather-moss
*Homalia trichomanoides*

Detail of leaves

**HABITAT** Woodland
**WHERE TO LOOK** Found on lower parts of tree trunks, especially ash, on calcareous and clay soils
**DESCRIPTION** An unusual, dark green moss, with long, flat shoots to 6cm long (and pressed leaves) which looks more like a liverwort at first glance; leaves (1.2mm long) rounded, translucent and overlapping, with a small nipple-like tip and faint nerve to half way along the leaf (seen through a hand lens); leaves loosely arch when dry, giving shoots a more cylindrical appearance; capsules egg-shaped
**SIMILAR SPECIES Flat Neckera** *Neckera complanata* (see p.57), found in similar situations, is a paler green

6mm

# Fox-tail Feather-moss
*Thamnobryum alopecurum*

Detail of scale-like stem leaves

**HABITAT** Woodland
**WHERE TO LOOK** A common moss of calcareous woodlands, in depressions, tree stumps and open soil
**DESCRIPTION** A large, distinctive, dark green, tree-like moss (8–15cm tall) with many branches at the shoot tips giving a small canopy-like appearance, when the moss is hanging from gradients it can look slightly different with spreading branches; main stem upright, rigid and branchless in the lower section; branch leaves (1.5–2.5mm long) egg-shaped with a toothed tip (seen through a hand lens)
**SIMILAR SPECIES Larger Mouse-tail Moss** *Isothecium alopecuroides* does not have toothed branch leaves

20mm

# Many-fruited Leskea
*Leskea polycarpa*

Capsules

3mm

**HABITAT** Flood zone of rivers and streams
**WHERE TO LOOK** A moss found in the flood zone of rivers and
streams, growing on branches, trunks and roots of trees, mud,
woodwork and concrete
**DESCRIPTION** A slender, dark yellow-green moss often flecked
with silty debris, forming branched patches with secondary
shoots (to 4mm long) standing erect or drooping; leaves (1mm
long) held pointing away from stem are rounded with a narrow
tip and a prominent nerve; capsules abundant, cylindrical, held
erect or slightly angled on an orange-brown seta
**SIMILAR SPECIES Creeping Feather-moss**
*Amblystegium serpens* (see p.61)
also produces abundant
capsules

6mm

# Rambling Tail-moss
*Anomodon viticulosus*

Detail of wet leaves

5mm

**HABITAT** Woodland, limestone rocks and walls
**WHERE TO LOOK** Found in calcareous woodland on banks and bases
of ash and field maple, also on shaded limestone rocks and walls
**DESCRIPTION** Large, yellow-green to bright green moss with erect
or drooping branches 2–8cm long (paler yellow-green shoot tips
contrast with green branches), often found on vertical surfaces;
leaves (2–3mm long) wide at base and blunt tipped with a
prominent nerve (seen through a hand lens); when dry, the
leaves are held tightly to the stem and look rope-like, but when
moistened, the leaves quickly spread out and
become a brighter green
**SIMILAR SPECIES** Unlikely to
be confused with
other species

8mm

# Common Tamarisk-moss
*Thuidium tamariscinum*

**HABITAT** Woodland and grassland
**WHERE TO LOOK** A very common moss growing over soil and
banks in woodland, also found on shaded grasslands
**DESCRIPTION** A very distinctive, large, yellow-green to dark green
moss with symmetrical, many-branched, feathery shoots
(making the moss look like a miniature fir tree or fern), with a
red, green or brown stem covered in thread-like, brown hairs;
branch leaves narrow and short (to 0.5mm long), stem leaves
much wider (1.5mm long), heart-shaped with a long curved tip
**SIMILAR SPECIES Philibert's Tamarisk-
moss** *Thuidium assimile* is shorter
and with less branches

Detail of leaves

25mm

# Curled Hook-moss
*Palustriella commutata*

**HABITAT** Fens and wet limestone
**WHERE TO LOOK** A rare moss of calcareous fens in Oxfordshire,
especially those near Abingdon
**DESCRIPTION** A large green, yellow or brown moss with
symmetrical, feather-like branches with a darker brown stem,
forming mats of shoots (4–6cm long) and often encrusted with
calcareous deposits making them feel hard; stem leaves (2–
2.5mm long) heart-shaped with a long, drawn-out tip, branch
leaves (to 1.5mm long) curved in a distinctive hook shape
**SIMILAR SPECIES Fern-leaved Hook-moss**
*Cratoneuron filicinum* has shorter
shoots and the leaves are
not as strongly curved

Detail of leaves

10mm

# Creeping Feather-moss
*Amblystegium serpens*

**HABITAT** Woodland and man-made habitats
**WHERE TO LOOK** A common moss growing on branches and fallen or decaying wood and twigs, also found near streams, rivers and other damp shaded places, and at bases of walls and on tarmac
**DESCRIPTION** A very fine and slender, branching, green to dark green moss, forming extensive patches of interweaving shoots (1–2cm long); stem leaves minute (0.5mm long), triangular with a long drawn out tip, branches thread-like; capsules common, yellow-green on a red seta; calyptra whitish-green
**SIMILAR SPECIES Willow Feather-moss**
*Hygroamblystegium varium*, found on wet or marshy ground, is slightly larger

Detail of moist leaves and capsules
2.5mm

8mm

# Yellow Starry Feather-moss
*Campylium stellatum*

**HABITAT** Wetlands, fens
**WHERE TO LOOK** An uncommon moss found in base-rich valley mires, fens and in wet depressions on Greenham Common
**DESCRIPTION** A medium-sized, yellow-green moss with erect, branching shoots 2–3cm long; leaves narrow and triangular (1.8–3mm long), gradually tapering to a sharp point, leaf tips are cylindrical in outline (seen through a hand lens) and spread away (almost at right-angles) from stem, giving the moss a starry appearance from above
**SIMILAR SPECIES Dull Starry Feather-moss**
*Campylium protensum*, locally abundant in fens, has much shorter, reclined shoots and dull green leaves

Detail of leaves
3mm

10mm

# Intermediate Hook-moss
*Scorpidium cossonii*

Detail of leaves

**HABITAT** Fens
**WHERE TO LOOK** A rare moss of calcareous fens in open, wet vegetation; key sites include Parsonage Moor and Dry Sandford Pit in Oxfordshire
**DESCRIPTION** A distinctive, medium-sized, slender, branching moss forming neat patches of erect, green and red-brown shoots; leaves strongly curved like a sickle (2–2.5mm long), all turned in the same direction
**SIMILAR SPECIES** **Ringless Hook-moss** *Sarmentypnum exannulatum* is found in wet heath and by acid or peaty pools

9mm

62

# Mouse-tail Moss
*Isothecium myosuroides*

Detail of leaves

**HABITAT** Woodland and rocky outcrops
**WHERE TO LOOK** A common moss found on vertical surfaces such as shaded mature tree trunks of ash, beech, oak and hazel; also found on boulders in shaded areas
**DESCRIPTION** A medium-sized, tree-like moss forming large mats, shoots (1–2cm long) growing horizontally erect with many branching tips, distinctively drooping downwards; branch leaves spearhead-shaped (2mm long), drawing to a sharply toothed point, spreading when moist, overlapping and slightly plaited when dry; capsules often present; calyptra claw-like
**SIMILAR SPECIES** **Larger Mouse-tail Moss** *Isothecium alopecuroides* has pointed, egg-shaped, concave leaves

5mm

# Silky Wall Feather-moss
## *Homalothecium sericeum*

**Detail of leaves**

4mm

**HABITAT** Rocky outcrops, man-made structures and woodland
**WHERE TO LOOK** Common on calcareous walls, roofs and
gravestones; also found as an epiphyte on ash, elder and willow
**DESCRIPTION** A medium-sized, yellow-green, branching moss,
with creeping branches clasping tightly to rocks and tree
stumps, and short secondary branches standing erect; leaves
pleated, spearhead-shaped, drawing to a point; leaves spread
out when moist, giving a star-like appearance, leaves and
secondary branches curl up tightly and appear wispy when dry
**SIMILAR SPECIES Yellow Feather-moss**
*Homalothecium lutescens*, found on
calcareous grassland, is more
yellow in colour

0mm

# Whitish Feather-moss
## *Brachythecium albicans*

**Detail of leaves**

2.5mm

**HABITAT** Grassland, heathland, quarries and disturbed habitats
**WHERE TO LOOK** A common moss found on eroded and disturbed
soils such as the edges of sandy paths, roads and waste ground;
also found in heath and unimproved lawns
**DESCRIPTION** Medium-sized moss with few branches, and whitish-
green to yellow-green string-like, cylindrical shoots that can be
erect, dropping or creeping; leaves (to 2mm long), overlapping,
rounded drawing to a long point which spreads away from
shoot; nerve to just over halfway (seen through a hand lens)
**SIMILAR SPECIES Streaky Feather-moss** *Brachythecium
glareosum* and **Sand Feather-moss**
*Brachythecium mildeanum* have
shoots not so string-like
in appearance

5mm

# Rough-stalked Feather-moss
*Brachythecium rutabulum*

Detail of capsule and seta

**HABITAT** A common moss of woodlands, wetlands and grasslands
**WHERE TO LOOK** Tree stumps, branches and over the ground in
    sheltered woodland, also found in damp grassland and lawns
**DESCRIPTION** Variable species with leaves loosely spread from
    branches, all softly directed towards the tip of the branch; the
    wrinkled, egg-shaped leaves draw to a short point and have a
    strong mid-vein ¾ along their length; wine red capsules often
    present with fine-grained dots running down the seta.
**SIMILAR SPECIES** **River Feather-moss** *Brachythecium
    rivulare*, found in wet woodland,
    has leaves less spreading
    and more compacted
    along its branches

6mm

# Neat Feather-moss
*Pseudoscleropodium purum*

Detail of leaves

**HABITAT** Grasslands, heathland, woodland and gardens
**WHERE TO LOOK** A common species in damp, unimproved
    grasslands, heath, and open woodland
**DESCRIPTION** Tall, yellow-green to green moss (up to 10cm tall)
    with regularly branching shoots, slightly translucent and
    succulent in appearance; leaves overlap and are wide, round
    and blunt with a small contracted tip (seen with a hand lens);
    branch leaves are similar to stem leaves
**SIMILAR SPECIES** **Red-stemmed Feather-moss** *Pleurozium
    schreberi* (see p.70), found on heathland and
    open heathy woodland, has red stems
    and more narrowly
    tapering leaves

6mm

# Hair-pointed Feather-moss
*Cirriphyllum piliferum*

**HABITAT** Broadleaved woodlands, stream banks and churchyards
**WHERE TO LOOK** Common on banks and on the ground in
woodlands and at the base of older walls in churchyards
**DESCRIPTION** A large, light to dark green moss (up to 10cm tall)
with regularly branching shoots along the main stem;
overlapping leaves are concave and oval, with a long, abruptly
contracting tip; shoot and branch tips are spear-shaped and
often a whitish green; the collected thread-like tips bend away
from the leaves at the shoot tips (visible through a hand lens)
**SIMILAR SPECIES** Unlikely to be confused
with other species

Detail of leaf tips

2mm

mm

65

# Common Striated Feather-moss
*Eurhynchium striatum*

**HABITAT** Broadleaved woodlands
**WHERE TO LOOK** On stumps and tree trunks and on the ground in
woodland
**DESCRIPTION** Pale or yellow-green mats, often with erect or
trailing tendrils; branches are often quite straight and appear
evenly spaced as they droop from low-cut stumps and tree
trunks; leaves heart-shaped (1.5–2mm long) with characteristic
wrinkles running parallel with the leaf nerve (visible through a
hand lens); capsules are occasionally present and have a red seta
**SIMILAR SPECIES** **Twist-tip Feather-moss** *Oxyrrhynchium
schleicheri*, found on loamy soil in woodland
in the Chilterns and a few sites in
Berks, has a twisted leaf tip

Detail of leaves

2.5mm

mm

# Common Feather-moss
*Kindbergia praelonga*

**HABITAT** Woodland and grassland
**WHERE TO LOOK** Very common in woodland on soil, decaying
wood, logs and tree trunks; also in damp lawns and grassland
**DESCRIPTION** Slender, pale green moss with regularly branching
stems, often seen drooping over logs and fallen branches, can
form large irregular blankets; leaves finely toothed (seen
through a hand lens), branch leaves heart-shaped with a
tapered tip turned to one side, stem leaves small and narrow
with straight tip; capsules common; calyptra curved and hooked
**SIMILAR SPECIES Swartz's Feather-moss**
*Oxyrrhynchium hians* has
branch and stem leaves
of the same shape

15mm

66

# Woodsy Silk-moss
*Plagiothecium nemorale*

**HABITAT** Woodland and hedgerows
**WHERE TO LOOK** Found on banks and damp, eroded edges in oak
and ash woodland, also on damp logs and tree trunks
**DESCRIPTION** Dark green moss which droops down from damp
surfaces; leaves (2–3mm long) flat (as if pressed), egg-shaped
with a narrowing tip, symmetrical, overlapping and angled
away from the stem at base
**SIMILAR SPECIES Juicy Silk-moss** *Plagiothecium succulentum* is
very similar but is more yellow-green; **Dentated Silk-moss**
*Plagiothecium denticulatum* and **Curved
Silk-moss** *Plagiothecium curvifolium*
have asymmetrical leaves

8mm

# Waved Silk-moss
*Plagiothecium undulatum*

**HABITAT** Acid woodland and conifer plantations
**WHERE TO LOOK** In conifer plantations and birch woodland on soil, leaf litter and tree stumps; more common in Berks
**DESCRIPTION** A large, pale white-green moss (10cm long) which droops down from damp surfaces; stems and leaves are flat as if they are pressed; leaves (3mm long) undulated (more obvious when dry) and overlapping
**SIMILAR SPECIES** Unlikely to be confused with other species

Detail of leaves

6mm

15mm

# Elegant Silk-moss
*Pseudotaxiphyllum elegans*

**HABITAT** Acid woodland and conifer plantations
**WHERE TO LOOK** Found on shaded, acidic soil, particularly on banks and eroded edges in woodlands and wooded lanes
**DESCRIPTION** A medium-sized, green to dark-green moss (3cm long) which droops down from damp banks; stems and leaves are flat as if they are pressed; leaves (1–1.5mm long) elongated, oval, drawing to a fine point; fine, hair-like, green branchlets often grow in abundance from leaf axils
**SIMILAR SPECIES** **Depressed Feather-moss** *Taxiphyllum wissgrillii* is found in woodland, often on flints, chalk and limestone fragments; *Plagiothecium* species (see p.66 and 67)

Detail of leaves and branchlets

3mm

6mm

# Pointed Spear-moss
*Calliergonella cuspidata*

**HABITAT** Grassland, fens and marshes, gardens
**WHERE TO LOOK** A very common moss of damp habitats, unimproved grassland and garden lawns
**DESCRIPTION** A branching, translucent, yellow-green moss with long shoots (3–8cm long) and pale brown to bright red stems (clearly seen through the leaves); shoot and branch tips terminate in a spear-shaped point of tightly compressed leaves (an important diagnostic feature); leaves large (2–2.5mm long), thick with a blunt tip
**SIMILAR SPECIES** Unlikely to be confused with other species

Detail of leaves

10mm

# Flat-brocade Moss
*Platygyrium repens*

**HABITAT** Damp woodland
**WHERE TO LOOK** An uncommon moss growing on bark of logs and trunks and branches of ash, alder, elder, hawthorn and willow
**DESCRIPTION** A small, slender, yellow-green to dark green moss with short, symmetrical branches (1cm tall) forming creeping mats with newer shoots standing erect away from the mat; leaves small (1–1.5mm long) and all tend to point in the same direction; shoot tip often with characteristic small branchlets which drop off the main plant helping it to reproduce
**SIMILAR SPECIES** **Supine Plait-moss** *Hypnum cupressiforme* var. *resupinatum* does not have small branchlets and is not held as tightly to the bark

Detail of deciduous branchlets

5mm

# Cypress-leaved Plait-moss
*Hypnum cupressiforme* var. *cupressiforme*

**HABITAT** Woodland, rocks
**WHERE TO LOOK** A very common moss found on bark of decaying wood, standing and fallen trees; also found on shaded rocks
**DESCRIPTION** A distinctive, but variable, green to brownish-green moss, with long or short shoots (to 2cm long), often trailing; leaves (1–2mm long) draw to a strongly curving point (often all turned in the same direction); leaves overlap tightly, giving a distinctive plaited look; capsules common
**SIMILAR SPECIES** **Great Plait-moss** *Hypnum cupressiforme* var. *lacunosum*, found on well-drained soils, is larger, with shorter orange-brown to greenish-brown shoots; **Mamillate Plait-moss** *Hypnum andoi* has longer, finer, trailing shoots

Detail of leaves

3mm

9mm

69

# Heath Plait-moss
*Hypnum jutlandicum*

**HABITAT** Woodland, conifer plantations and heathland
**WHERE TO LOOK** On open soil in acid woodland and ageing heathlands; often found beside tree trunks and where water run-off is frequent
**DESCRIPTION** One of the smaller plait-mosses (shoots 2–3cm long) with branches often symmetrical and evenly divided, and a distinctive silvery grey-green hue to its leaves and a green stem; leaves (2mm long) nerveless, with tips curling back on themselves, have the distinctive plaiting of the *Hypnum* genus
**SIMILAR SPECIES** Unlikely to be confused with other species

Detail of leaves and green stem

5mm

5mm

# Comb-moss
## *Ctenidium molluscum*

Detail of leaves

**HABITAT** Calcareous grasslands and woodlands, quarries and fens
**WHERE TO LOOK** A moss with a strong preference for calcareous conditions, found in open grassland, woodland banks, quarries and fens
**DESCRIPTION** Grows in yellow-green wefts, with shoots 2–3cm long, often with metallic-like highlights to the leaves; main stem is often a darker ginger-brown in colour, side branches grow opposite each other along the stem; leaves (1–2mm long) overlap along the branches and are very tufted, curled or wisped, giving the moss a very distinctive look
**SIMILAR SPECIES** Unlikely to be confused with other species

10mm

# Red-stemmed Feather-moss
## *Pleurozium schreberi*

Detail of leaves

**HABITAT** Acid grassland, heathland, open acid woodland and bogs
**WHERE TO LOOK** Found on acid grassland, at the edges of heathy woodland, amongst heather in heathland and bogs
**DESCRIPTION** This distinctive, pinnately branched, robust moss (5–10cm tall) has yellow-green, translucent leaves and a prominent blood-red stem; leaves (2–2.5mm long) overlap and are inflated, oval and blunt tipped
**SIMILAR SPECIES** **Neat Feather-moss** *Pseudoscleropodium purum* (see p.64), found in a wider range of grassy habitats, has pointed leaf tips and lacks the red stem

10mm

# Big Shaggy-moss
*Rhytidiadelphus triquetrus*

**HABITAT** Woodland and chalk grassland
**WHERE TO LOOK** This moss grows on calcareous soils in woodland, scrub, chalk grassland, roadside verges and in churchyards
**DESCRIPTION** This large and robust moss has long shoots (5–20cm long) with drooping, irregular branches and a red to orange (more obvious when wet) stem; leaves spread away from stem and branches in all directions; leaves pleated (up to 6mm long), pale, rounded at base and draw to a point, with teeth present along the leaf tip (seen through a hand lens)
**SIMILAR SPECIES** The rare **Little Shaggy-moss** *Rhytidiadelphus loreus* is much more slender and is found on acidic soils

Detail of leaves

5mm

20mm

# Springy Turf-moss
*Rhytidiadelphus squarrosus*

**HABITAT** Grasslands, lawns and heathland
**WHERE TO LOOK** A very common moss found in lawns and a range of unimproved or semi-improved grasslands (more abundantly in shorter turfs where grazing or mowing regularly takes place), also found in grassy heathland
**DESCRIPTION** A robust moss (up to 15cm long, but usually much shorter) with translucent yellow-green leaves and a prominent red stem; shoots do not obviously branch and often droop over vegetation or stand erect; leaves distinctive (2–2.5mm long), bend away from the stem until they are pointing down the stem, giving a star-like appearance from above
**SIMILAR SPECIES** Unlikely to be confused with other species

Detail of leaves

2mm

5mm

# Species index

**73**

# Recommended books

his book with its 219 species mentioned is just an introduction to the many more mosses and liverworts found
n Berkshire, Buckinghamshire and Oxfordshire. If you want to know more about mosses and liverworts then the
ooks below are recommended.

*Mosses and liverworts of Britain and Ireland; a field guide* (2010) edited by Ian Atherton, Sam Bosanquet and Mark
awley. Published by the British Bryological Society. ISBN 978 0 9561310 1 0 – A photographic field guide
overing over 800 species, with detailed identification notes and distribution maps. Uses the recommended
nglish names.

*Arable bryophytes* (2008) by Ron Porley. Published by WILDGuides. ISBN 978 1 903657 21 8 – A field guide to the
mosses, liverworts and hornworts of cultivated land in Britain and Ireland. With detailed identification notes,
olour photographs and line drawings.

*British mosses and liverworts* 3rd edition (1988) by E. V. Watson. Published by Cambridge University Press.
SBN 0 521 28536 4 – An introduction to mosses and liverworts, with descriptions, ecological details and line
drawings of the commoner and more notable species.

From balloons and bristles to pincushions and plaits, there's an intriguing world of tiny plants waiting to be discovered. This pocket guide to mosses and liverworts found in Berkshire, Buckinghamshire and Oxfordshire helps you to identify many of the fascinating micro-plants that grow in towns, parks, woodland and nature reserves.

This guide focuses on the species most likely to be found by the beginner, b[ut] it also includes striking, rarer examples from the local area.

Covering over 200 species and fully illustrated with beautiful photographs throughout, it includes easy-to-follow descriptions, ideal for those wanting [to] find out more about the micro world all around them. Information on key habitats and the best places to look, is also provided.

**Other guides in the series
from Pisces Publications**

*A guide to finding fungi
in Berkshire, Buckinghamshire & Oxfordshire*
ISBN 978 1 874357 38 4

*A guide to finding orchids
in Berkshire, Buckinghamshire & Oxfordshire*
ISBN 978 1 874357 57 5

piscespublications

ISBN 978-1-874357-56-8

9 781874 357568